JUSTICE AT WORK

JUSTICE AT WORK

GLOBALIZATION
AND THE HUMAN
RIGHTS OF WORKERS

ROBERT A. SENSER

To order additional copies of this book, contact:
Xlibris Corporation
1-888-795-4274
www.Xlibris.com
Orders@Xlibris.com
55666

CONTENTS

for my wife

Dzung Senser

WANTING TO GO HOME
Garment Worker in Bangladesh
(see "On Their Knees," page 18)

CHAPTER 1

Where I'm Coming From

FROM ONE ANGLE, my professional career looks like a string of jobs with nothing in common except paychecks. In a lifetime of working in the public and private sectors on four continents, I've been a butcher shop helper, a clerk typist, a soldier, a reporter, an editor, a staff member of a Catholic organization, a Foreign Service officer, and a program director for a foreign assistance organization.

If all those jobs—excepting the short-termers and forty-two months in the army—had to fit under one heading, it would be this: writer. Starting in high school, I found that I liked to write and that others liked what I wrote. It is a skill that served me mighty well, especially in my tours as a U.S. labor attaché in Algiers, Bonn, Brussels, and Saigon during my twenty-one years in the Foreign Service.

My father had hopes that I would follow in his footsteps by making an honest living as a shoe repairman, like his father before him. As a head start, he got me a Saturday job wrapping repaired shoes in a Chicago department store where he knew the manager. It was fast-paced work. Shoes of all sorts kept piling up, and you had to wrap them quickly to keep the pile down and the customers happy. Twice, or maybe three times, I wrapped together two shoes that looked alike but were not a pair. Customers do not like it when they get home and find they have two shoes, only one of which is theirs. The manager didn't like it either. He let me go home early, saying I didn't have to return the next Saturday.

Dad kept trying. I lasted longer at another Saturday job he lined up, this time in a department store butcher shop as all-around handyman doing chores in and out of a below-freezing meat locker. It was an environment that I did not warm up to. That summer, when school was out, I helped build a cistern, repair a badly leaking roof, waterproof our basement, and dig a drainage ditch—labor useful as an apprenticeship for a career in residential construction. But that too was not to be. What led me astray was a high school typing class.

Yes, an ordinary touch-typing class started me down a long road that, decades later, led me to write and edit this book. The nun who taught my typing class at Cardinal Stritch High School in Chicago was doing research on Dante for her master's degree, and she asked me to take the streetcar trip to pick up books for her at the central library. Not often, but each time was an adventure. On one afternoon trip downtown, I stopped by a large bookstore (large for the time) and became fascinated by the colorful array of magazines from all over the world. Among the many temptations, I settled on the magazine *Writer's Digest*. Its cover was a purple so lurid I hid the magazine under a living room carpet when I got home. I read it studiously. It listed dozens and dozens of publications actually open to publishing what I wrote.

One evening, in bed with the flu, I was scanning the *Chicago Daily News* when I noticed a fascinating story about a blind Boy Scout troop with a blind scoutmaster. Bingo! I quickly called him for an interview—my first ever. When the scoutmaster came to the phone, he listened and asked, "How old are you?" I couldn't disguise that I was sixteen. Still, I got my interview, wrote my article, put it in proper form (as per *Writer's Digest* guidance), and mailed it off, with a proper cover letter (again as per), to *This Week* magazine, then a national Sunday supplementary section for the *Daily News*. Soon I found a thin envelope addressed to me in the mailbox on our front porch. It was an offer to buy not the article, but the article *idea* for $35. That was a little disappointing at first. As it turned out, however, *This Week* published my work in its October 1, 1938, issue under a joint byline, mine and that of a *Daily News* reporter who had beefed it up (but kept my title, "Scouts Courageous," and my opening paragraphs about the Scouts saluting a flag they could not see). It looked impressive pinned on the high school bulletin board.

A schoolmate, looking up at the article with my sister, asked, "Your brother wrote this?"

"He can write anything," my sister said. I thought so too in those days. And soon I was off on a new writing venture.

One warm afternoon, when my father was supposed to be on the job working in a downtown shoe repair shop, he swung open the screen door on the back porch, rushed past me, saying only, "I got fired."

Unemployment was not a new experience for him, or us. Years earlier, our lives were disrupted when Dad lost his job at a shoe repair shop in South Chicago's Pullman Car Works, which shut down because of the Depression. But this was different. It was a union official who got him fired.

As my father gradually told me the whole story, I got angrier and angrier. I let off steam on my new Corona portable, which my parents had purchased so that I wouldn't borrow one from a girl in my high school class. I tapped out an article about my father's fate and his reactions to it, all in the first person (Dad writing anonymously). Weeks later, it appeared in the February 2, 1940, issue of *Commonweal* under the title "Appeal of a Catholic Workman" and the subtitle "A Human Document That Vividly Describes the Effect of Labor Racketeering on the Rank and File."

It was indeed vivid but didn't quite deliver all that the subtitle promised. Rather, my account focused on the abuses committed in one local union and the injustice inflicted on one worker, my father, and his family. The article led off with a series of dramatic comments by five unnamed workers indicting unions in general. One quote was "Unions are all a racket." Another: "If this isn't the shortest way to communism, I don't know what is." After the quotes came a colorful generalization by my father (really me): "As ominously as the rumble of thunder, remarks like these can be heard wherever working men gather." A few paragraphs later, the article contradicted the hyperbole by asserting, "The men do not grumble at the idea of a union as such . . . [but] against the perceived laxity of national union headquarters in their supervision of locals." (The adjective *perceived* was added by the editors, I'm sure; it wasn't yet a part of my vocabulary.)

My father's story had an unexpected ending. After a year or so doing odd jobs, he again got full-time work in a unionized downtown repair shop, and he gladly rejoined the local union, even with the same official at the head. His perspective remained as expressed in our article: "I know, from the [popes'] social encyclicals, that the idea of unionism is sound. As a result, I don't condemn unions: I condemn the way they're administered."

That experience was an early expression of sensitivity to the plight of the vulnerable. It flowed from the gut instinct of a human rights advocate—a term also not yet a part of my vocabulary.

Thank God, most of my paid employment over the years was congenial to that instinct. Indeed, it was an unwritten job requirement for editing *Work*, published by the Catholic Council on Working Life in Chicago, where I worked for seventeen years before joining the Foreign Service. For example, I ghosted a series of first-person articles based on interviews with ordinary people—a black couple whose suburban home had been burned down by racists, a steelworker who defended the grievances of his fellow workers, a stockyard worker who made her living packing pigs' feet. Occasionally, I traveled to research special stories as a freelance writer. The *New Republic*, in its December 5, 1955, issue published my article, "Hunting Elephants with Popguns," describing the frustrations of organizing workers in the rice mills of southern Louisiana.

While a program director for an affiliate of the American Federation of Labor and Congress of Industrial Organizations (AFL-CIO), the Asian-American Free Labor Institute, in Washington, D.C., I again freelanced in late 1996 by sending *Foreign Affairs* a suggestion for article on workers in China, even though I had not yet been to China's mainland. The article idea blossomed into an article occupying fourteen pages in the March/April 1997 issue of *Foreign Affairs,* "China's Troubled Workers," by Anita Chan and Robert A. Senser. It was the product of an unusual transpacific collaboration conducted entirely through the Internet, based largely on field research conducted by Dr. Chan, a sociologist at Australian National University, and scholars whose studies she had translated.

So it was that my articles appeared in an assortment of national publications, usually small ones. I would become intrigued by a subject—corporate social responsibility, for example—and then after compiling a stack of research, would write a lengthy article that I'd send, unsolicited, to a magazine most likely to print it—the quarterly *Dissent* in this instance. From the selection in this book, you can see that my writings often found a home in *America,* a weekly published by Jesuits in New York City. I'm especially grateful to them for accepting my articles on the need for trade reform, which the nation's dailies oppose stridently on their editorial pages and quietly on their news pages.

In February 1996, anxious to have my own media outlet for writing on matters that intrigue me, I launched my own Web site, Human Rights for Workers, which in early 2008 mutated into a blog, Human Rights for Workers. This book weaves selections from them together with selected magazine articles on human rights issues that excited me the most during the past seventeen years.

Another Me

I HESITATED TO bring up another aspect of my life, but here goes. The Lewis and Clark expedition has long fascinated me. That fascination increased when I read Stephen Ambrose's best-selling book, *Undaunted Courage,* on its exploits. In fact, I bought some maps on which I started tracking the routes that the expedition, officially called the Corps of Discovery, took by boat, horse, and foot nearly two centuries ago. I felt I was there beside them, exploring the huge territory of the Pacific Northwest. I once checked out tours that retrace parts of that perilous journey. I never did so in person.

Somehow, though, I executed a conceptual leap and began reflecting on the intellectual journey I had taken during decades of writing (under my name, under others', and under none) magazine articles, op-ed pieces, speeches, memos, brochures, pamphlets, press releases, talking points, and briefing papers on various topics, particularly human rights. How might I characterize all that work? Outlandish as it first sounded, the question hit me: could someone in a role like mine—could I—be considered an explorer?

It had never been in my job description. What, except for self-flattery, led me to believe that it fit me now? How could I think that my mundane endeavors are somehow remotely comparable to those of the Lewis and Clark pioneers? I don't face their perilous obstacles. I can't claim to have the courage remotely like theirs. And even within my own field of endeavor, I certainly haven't achieved the success they did.

Still, for years now, I have felt that the characteristic inherent in *exploring* fits at least my best work. Longer than I realized, I have indeed been on a challenging intellectual journey, venturing into new territory—globalization. Longer than I realized, I have been exploring a world that is substantially different from the world of a half century ago, different in kind and not just in degree, a world transformed by an explosive growth in trade, investment, technology, and communication.

What helped me pursue this line of inquiry was a book, *Global Public Policy: Governing Without Government?* by Wolfgang H. Reinicke, then a senior scholar at Brookings Institution, which published the book in 1998. For me, Reinicke's key insight was this: there is a fundamental difference between international interdependence and globalization. Briefly, economic interdependence refers only to a *quantitative* intensification of economic activities between *countries*. Globalization, on the other hand, is distinguished by a *qualitative* change marked by the integration of the structure and behavior of *corporations* into the international economy.

I read and reread the book and was so excited by it that, without a commission to do so, I wrote a review that the U.S. Department of Labor *Monthly Labor Review* published in its January 1999 issue. I include it in a chapter in this book, "Global Insights," along with my review of another economist's book.

Indeed, much of my writing of the past sixteen or seventeen years deals, directly or indirectly, with globalization as illuminated by Reinicke. That is so for much of the work that appears in this book. I explore twenty-first-century globalization on four levels: 1) how it affects the lives of working men, women, and children; 2) how institutions such as the World Trade Organization deal or don't deal with that challenge; 3) how the prevailing paradigm for the world economy needs to change: and 4) what people can do to change it. I can't claim any great scientific breakthroughs. But I have tried to throw light on the globalization as it is and as it ought to be.

More Editorial Notes

I DON'T LIKE truncated statistics. When I wrote about the value of goods imported into the United States from China for the whole of 2007, for example, I didn't write that it reached "$321.5 billion, an increase of $33.7 billion over 2006." Instead I wrote, "$321,500,000,000, an increase of $33,700,000,000 over 2006."

The press releases of the Census Bureau use the abbreviated form. So do newspapers and magazines. In fact, some go further, shrinking billion into *b*, million into *m*. The full figures take too much space. They don't fit into a one-column headline. As a result, readers don't fully grasp the vastness not only of our trade deficits but also of our national debt, our federal budget, and many other statistical indices of our national health. Books aren't faced with that constraint. So in these pages, I make use of my wider freedom here.

Something else you may notice about this book is that it has a certain amount of repetition. This is not a careless error. It is done on purpose, in two ways:

I favor certain economists because of the clarity and wisdom of their writings. I am not inhibited about repeatedly drawing on the insights of three of them in particular—Wolfgang Reinicke, Dani Rodrik, and Joseph Stiglitz.

Specific subjects also recur in these pages, deliberately so. Two examples are intellectual property protections and investment protections, which surface in several chapters. I resisted deleting duplications because they are not, in my view, pure redundancies. The two subjects play important roles in globalization, and over the years, I have paid a lot of attention to controversies that rage about them. This book partially reflects that concentration, hopefully to enhance the reader's understanding of issues neglected in media reporting.

The overall purpose of this book is the same as the purpose of my Web site and Weblog, Human Rights for Workers. It is to describe how globalization affects working men and women and how it creates the need to integrate human rights, including the human rights of workers, into global rules and practices at the national, regional, and international levels through governmental, quasi-governmental, private business, labor union, and other channels. That purpose requires a vision—a vision different from the one that inspired the policies that shape today's globalization.

After the cold war ended, the United States as the sole superpower was in the unprecedented position of being able to shape the global economy. In a 2003 interview conducted by the Carnegie Council for Ethics in International Affairs, Joseph Stiglitz, the Nobel Prize-winning economist, described how the United States mishandled that opportunity. It could have tried "to create an international economic order based on principles like social justice, fairness between developed and less developed countries," but it lacked the vision based on those principles, Stiglitz said. "The financial and commercial sector in the United States did have a vision. They might not believe in government having an active role, except when it advanced their interest. The active role they pushed for was to gain market access, to push an agenda that advanced our [own narrow] interests . . . [instead of] trying to create a fair international economic order."

What is the vision that most inspires my work? I have often meditated on that question. In my best moments, I find inspiration in the Bible, all the way back to Genesis. The Bible's first pages proclaim twice (just to be sure that we don't miss the point) that God created human beings in his own image and likeness. You and I, every one of us, bears the image and likeness of God in our very being. Is there, can there be, a more profound basis for respecting the human rights of every human being and for challenging violations of those rights? Our origin has implications that are staggering. We mere human beings, all of us, are blessed with a divine imprint. I continue to search for what that profound truth means for us today, individually and for society at large.

My favorite biblical quotation is from the First Psalm, paraphrased as *Happy indeed is the person who delights in the words of the Lord and who grows in wisdom by pondering their meaning for us day and night.*

CHAPTER 2

On Their Knees

I had seen many photographs of child labor, starting with the historic ones taken in U.S. mines and textile mills during the early 1900s. But these disturbing images did not prepare me for the shock of personally seeing little girls and boys toiling in factories. That happened to me on a visit to Bangladesh garment factories during a reporting trip to Asia in 1991. I recounted that experience in the article below, published in the September 19, 1992, issue of *America* magazine. "On Their Knees" was among my first writings on the plight of working men, women, and children in the global economy.

IT IS ONLY A POSTER, but the boy it pictures haunts me. His forlorn eyes stare at me from the wall across the room in my home office. He looks out from behind an iron gate, his hands gripping the bars. He is kneeling on his bare knees. For me, the position of that boy—on his knees—has become a metaphor for the plight of countless boys and girls working in the factories of Bangladesh and other Asian countries producing goods for the world market.

Although I have seen many dozens of those working children and interviewed some of them, I never met the boy in the poster, a dark-faced Bangladeshi child of eight or nine whom I call Ali. I first saw Ali in a color slide that had been taken by a Bangladeshi human rights activist, Rosaline Costa. When I borrowed the slide to enlarge it into the poster, Ms. Costa told me the story behind it.

She works for the Commission for Justice and Peace of the Catholic Bishops' Conference of Bangladesh. One hot summer afternoon in the capital city, Dhaka, she was walking down a street lined with multistoried warrens that house garment factories. As usual, the collapsible iron gates at the factory entrances were all pulled shut and locked. Here and there, security guards lingered in the shadows as added insurance against forbidden movement in or out of the busy plants.

Behind one of those gates, Rosaline Costa noticed a strange figure—the boy I call Ali. Kneeling there, on the verge of tears, he was begging the security guard to let him go home. The guard, muttering words of disapproval, ordered the boy to go back to work. Ms. Costa snapped Ali's picture before he rose and returned to the factory.

The photograph is unusual; the plight it depicts is not. Children are employed throughout Bangladesh's booming export garment industry. These children, younger than fourteen years of age, made up at least 15 percent of its workforce of four hundred thousand to five hundred thousand. In one sense, Ali is not typical of those children. The great majority of them are girls. Garment employers prefer young female workers because they are considered more docile and more nimble-fingered than males.

Some of the children are as young as seven. They work on the same schedule as adults—at least six days a week, often seven days a week, from seven or eight in the morning until the late afternoon or evening. Occasionally, to fill rush seasonal orders, they work all through the night for as much as thirty-six hours straight. They help make pajamas, blouses, shirts, and other clothes for costumers in the United States, Canada, and Europe.

Reading about their situation in research reports—and there are many—is shocking enough. It is even more shocking to see the children at work and to talk with them directly as I have done on two trips to Dhaka.

Their presence in the garment and other industries is not clandestine. The government's periodic labor force surveys routinely list statistics on employed children as young as five. In the three Dhaka factories I visited, I saw so many child workers that I hesitated to quiz the managers about them, lest I cause trouble for Ms. Costa, my Bangladeshi escort. In a tour of one factory, the manager and I paused near a group of youths who seemed to be under ten years old. Affecting my best nonjudgmental tone, I wondered whether the workers in the group might be as young as twelve.

"Yes," he said, "some eight or nine." Then, perhaps noting something in my facial expression, he quickly added, "They need the work."

Among the factory's three hundred workers, largely women, there were at least fifty children who in the opinion of my escort looked to be under fifteen, as well as many more aged fifteen through eighteen. It was numbing to watch the little ones—children who, instead of studying in a grade school classroom, were busy in a factory making clothes for distant consumers, among them little American schoolchildren of their own age. We had no trouble getting the manager's permission to take photographs in that factory, although we refrained from talking with any of the closely supervised children.

Because of a chance encounter at a Dhaka training seminar, I was able to conduct interviews of more than an hour and a half in September 1991 with two sisters—one, eleven; the other, ten—who personalized some of the stories that I had read and heard. I thought that the girls, speaking through an interpreter, would be shy; but they weren't and cheerfully agreed to do a rerun of the interview for my video camera. It was a Friday, the weekly legal holiday. Normally, they would have been working eight hours that Friday, but they were off because their factory was closed for major repairs. On the other six days of the week, they work a longer schedule, from 7 a.m. to as late as 10 p.m. As all-around helpers, the older girl earns the equivalent of $9 a month; the younger, $7. Though it was nearly the end of September, they had not yet collected their pay even for August.

It was the second factory job for the older girl. At a prior job she sometimes had to work from 8 a.m. till six the next morning, with only short breaks for rest and food. When she got sick on this schedule and declined to continue to work through the night, she was fired without being able to collect her final month's pay.

The two sisters confirmed what I had learned elsewhere—that management commonly relies on physical punishment to enforce discipline. They said that their male supervisors routinely subject children to blows to the head for making "mistakes," such as miscounts in packing or unpacking. In other kinds of punishment, children, as well as young women, are forced to kneel on the floor for ten to thirty minutes or to stand on their head for a long time.

From destinations listed on packing crates and from the brand names on labels, they know that all the clothes they work on are for export. Recently, they were putting pajamas for two- to five-year-olds into crates bound for New York City.

The situation described by the two sisters, far from being exceptional, is the normal pattern in Bangladesh's export garment sector, the country's largest industry. But isn't child labor against the law in Bangladesh? Yes, very much so. The Factory Act specifically prohibits the employment of any child under fourteen in factories. That prohibition, conforming to an International Labor Organization (ILO) convention that Bangladesh has ratified, is flagrantly violated. So is a Factory Act provision restricting the employment of youngsters fourteen through seventeen to no more than five hours a day and never between 7 p.m. and 7 a.m. There is no law or ILO convention against the physical punishment of child workers.

Starting in 1985, when the bishops' Commission for Justice and Peace conducted a survey of one thousand garment workers, study after study, one by the Bangladesh government itself in 1989, have documented these abuses. But nothing has changed, except that as Bangladesh's garment exports increase, so does child labor.

The problem attracts special press attention in Dhaka from time to time when child workers are the victims of factory fires or accidents. The worst recent tragedy, even noted briefly by the *New York Times*, occurred on the morning of December 27, 1990, in Dhaka's Sharaka garments factory, where a sudden fire killed the manager and twenty-four workers and injured at least one hundred. Of the twenty-four dead workers, eleven were under sixteen years old; three were girls twelve years of age. (Two of the survivors later told an interviewer that the factory regularly employed children as young as seven.) Most of the dead were found at a ground-floor exit, where a collapsible iron gate stayed closed for deadly minutes until firemen could force it open.

News of the tragedy at Sharaka sparked rage in a normally quiescent workforce. In the weeks of wildcat strikes and unrest that followed, about sixty garment factories suffered property damage because of sabotage, according to garment employers, who, unlike their workers, are well organized in the Bangladesh Garment Manufacturers and Exporters Association. Once again, the government launched a study. It even appointed a minimum wage board for the industry, hardly a bold initiative, since most garment factories have yet to implement the minimum rates that a previous board established seven years ago.

I visited the headquarters of the association to see what the Bangladeshi factory owners had to say for themselves. The association president, Mohammad Mosharraf Hossain, and four fellow officers were kind enough to receive me and (in fluent English) review the garment industry situation. Although the discussion on child labor revealed nothing new, it was interesting to get their views.

First of all, there was denial. Child labor? No, not in the garment factories.

What about photographs showing children at work? Those children only *seem* young, especially to Westerners. Malnutrition from early childhood adds to the false impression.

In the give-and-take that followed, the association officers retreated to the admission that some young children are indeed present in the plants, but only because mothers working there don't want to leave them at home. Under the circumstances, what could a factory manager do? (I forgot to say that, in compliance with the law, they could set up a day nursery.) Then, they argued that it is wrong to apply Western values to the situation. Bangladesh's practices emanate from the country's own culture, they said, and should not be judged by standards of another culture.

A familiar theme, and I was gad to deal with it. Sticking to your own cultural ways, I said, might work when you're producing only for your domestic market. But the whole purpose of your export industry is to produce for the world, and when you choose to be part of the global economy, you can expect that some other standards will come into play. For example, if U.S. families learn that the made-in-Bangladesh clothes they buy for their children are made by Bangladesh children of the same age, they might well have a negative reaction based on their own values.

Besides, I continued, Bangladesh is making a mistake in its economic development strategy by taking the traditional standards that exist in its impoverished agricultural economy and transferring them to its thriving modern sector, to the detriment of the country's women and children. Nor should you expect to keep your child labor a secret from American television. I pointed out that Harry Wu, under assignment from CBS, had recently succeeded in penetrating China's prison camps and photographing prisoners making goods for export to the United States.

The group listened courteously to this explanation, even to my recapitulation for the benefit of a board member who had missed key points because of a phone call. Then I gently introduced a new issue by congratulating them on their success in organizing their own association of private employers. It is a basic right to which you are certainly entitled, I said, but so are the workers in their industry. This struck a nerve, and they reacted strongly, more so than to any previous comment of mine.

"Why," one said heatedly, "in my factory I have set up a provident fund."

As others began chiming in, voices rising, the president, Mr. Hossain, took over and quietly pointed out that the law of Bangladesh guarantees the right to form unions. True, but then why, I asked (without bringing up a recently publicized case), do hooligans beat up women garment workers who try to organize unions?

I didn't make any converts, didn't expect to. As proved by the fact sheets they gave me, they have a good thing going, and so why should they change? Any pressure from the United States or Europe to restrict child labor imports is rejected as "protectionism," and protectionism of course is a modern sacrilege. So, thanks to the unprecedented opportunities in the international marketplace, the shipments from Bangladesh factories have turned the country into the seventh largest supplier of garments to the United States, ninth largest to Canada, tenth largest to the European Community. The number of workers in the industry, listed as over four hundred thousand on one fact sheet, has now grown to five hundred thousand, I was told. More and more little Alis will be pulled into the industrial labor force if, as one fact sheet foresees, the number of garment factories more than doubles from the present 850.

The industry is a "bright spot" in the Bangladesh economy, says a U.S. Embassy report distributed by the U.S. Labor Department. As confirming evidence, the *Wall Street Journal* (August 6, 1991) pointed to the many new jobs created by the industry and cited the case of one husband proud of the garment factory jobs of his four wives, which the article noted is "the maximum allowed under the country's Islamic law."

A political analyst, Francis Fukuyama, writes in his new book, *The End of History and the Last Man*, "All countries undergoing economic modernization must increasingly resemble one another." The question is whether, in the modernizing dynamics of the global economy, Bangladesh will develop so as to resemble the United States or the other way around. The outlook is far from bright.

Some months later, my warning about the investigative power of American TV came true in Bangladesh. Following up on my information, a *Dateline NBC* camera crew visited Dhaka and didn't even need to rely on a hidden camera for their story. They toured two garment factories and readily got permission to use a home video camera. As a result, nearly 14,000,000 American households saw vivid images of how Bangladesh's booming garment industry employed underage children by the tens of thousands, mostly girls. The children, busy helping produce shirts for U.S. stores, including Wal-Mart, said that they earned $12 to $20 a month, or 5¢ to 8¢ an hour, and were kept locked in at the plants until they met the day's production quota, sometimes well past midnight. One nine-year-old girl, who had been working at the plant for six months, pleaded with Rosaline Costa, the crew's escort-interpreter: "Please, can you take me with you? I don't want to stay here anymore."

CHAPTER 3

The Crime of Child Slavery

It is often assumed that the revulsion against abusive child labor springs from Western values alone. Not so. In fact, one of the world's powerful voices for the rights of children has been an Asian, Kailash Satyarthi. And the leading debunker of myths about child labor, an American political scientist, the late Myron Weiner, based his findings on firsthand research (his own and others') in India and other Asian countries. I quoted Satyarthi and Weiner in many of the articles I've written over the years, including "Outlawing the Crime of Child Labor" (below), which first appeared in the November-December 1993 issue of *Freedom Review*, published by Freedom Foundation. The crime lives on in many forms as illustrated in two other articles in this chapter.

"WHO SAYS SLAVERY is dead? It is still very much alive. It survives especially among children—more than 200,000,000 in the world, very many of them Asians."

The speaker is a charismatic Asian in his late thirties, a Brahmin by birth, an engineer by training, and a social activist by choice. Kailash Satyarthi has a simple message, one that he is promulgating across the world, from the small villages of his native India to the power centers of Washington, London, and Frankfurt: it is time to liberate the millions of children now held in servitude.

Satyarthi chairs the South Asian Coalition on Child Servitude, a network of more than sixty nongovernmental groups trying to free South Asian children from slavery and near slavery. On September 18, 1993, Satyarthi escorted about 250 children, most of them aged from six to twelve, in a march through the streets of New Delhi to protest the employment of children in sweatshops. The little marchers chanted, "We want our freedom," and carried banners reading Stop Buying and Selling Products Made by Children, Replace Children with Millions of Unemployed Adults, and Let There Be Free, Compulsory Education for All. In a sit-down in front of the Labor Ministry, they displayed a few of the products Indian children make—glass bangles, household locks, brassware, and bricks.

Satyarthi introduced reporters to some of the marchers. One of them, fourteen-year-old Devandandan, had been rescued from forced labor in a carpet factory a few months earlier. He said that in 1991 he was coaxed to leave home by promises of wages up to $100 a month for working at a loom two hours a day while going to school. Instead, he was forced to work, eat, and sleep locked in the same room, knotting carpets from 4 a.m. till late evening for pennies a day.

The demonstration was part of the annual Day Against Child Servitude, observed in India since 1989 on the first anniversary of a Pakistani Supreme Court decision that led to releasing hundreds of children from bondage. Protests less dramatic than the one in New Delhi were held in other South Asian cities, as well as in a few other European cities. In the United States, demonstrators picketed fourteen Wal-Mart stores nationwide to protest the chain's record of purchasing garments from Asian suppliers notorious for employing girls and boys under fourteen six and seven days a week.

The observances were a few recent public signs of a fledgling international movement against an ancient evil commonly called child labor. Although South Asia by no means has a monopoly on the labor of children, the worst and most numerous abuses are concentrated there, even in organized commercial industries making carpets, glassware, shoes, fireworks, locks, and other products. South Asians themselves are leading the crusade against the evil they call child servitude. Once dismissed as unrealistic dreamers, they have now won unprecedented national and international attention to their cause.

According to the view that predominated until recently, child labor is so endemic in the developing world that realistically you can't abolish it; you can only ameliorate the children's working conditions. Instead of trying to remove children from sweatshops, you make sure that if they lose a finger on the job, they get proper medical care before they go back to work again in, hopefully, a safer environment.

That approach is fatalistic and ignores the realities of child labor. Actually, the term *child labor* is too benign for the fate of most children who work full-time in industry, certainly in India's carpet-weaving and glassmaking plants. The term as commonly used covers

— at one extreme, the suburban U.S. high school student who holds a part-time job in a fast-food outlet and illegally works past 7 p.m. on a school day; and
— at the other extreme, the low-caste Indian boy aged ten kidnapped from his home, forced to work in a carpet factory many miles away from his home, and beaten if he cries for his mother.

Applied to a wide range of practices, the same term implies that the harmful practices it covers are reprehensible to a roughly equal extent when they actually are not. Still, the Anti-Slavery International of London has argued that any child conscripted into the full-time labor force before a certain age (say fourteen or fifteen) and thus deprived of their right to an education is suffering a contemporary form of slavery.

Cultural relativism condemns such judgmental language. The governments of China, Malaysia, and Singapore have taken the lead in rejecting the imposition of what they call "Western values."

But Asian voices like that of Satyarthi insist that their cause is one in defense of universal values.

Another rationale, popular even among Washington policymakers, is that no progress on eliminating child labor will occur until poverty declines. "But we argue the other way," Satyarthi told a session at the 1993 UN Conference on Human Rights in Vienna. "Today, in India, we have 55,000,000 children in servitude and an equal number of unemployed adults. No government can scale down unemployment without curbing child labor," which, he insists, perpetuates poverty.

No foreigner has done more research on child labor in India than Professor Myron Weiner, director of the Center for International Studies at MIT. In his book, *The Child and the State in India,* he documents the corrosive effect of the view that children in the lower castes or classes, starting as early as the age of five, are *meant* to work rather than to study. "India's low per capita income and economic situation," he writes, "is less relevant as an explanation [of child servitude] than the belief systems of the state bureaucracy . . . widely shared by educators, social scientists, trade unionists, and, more broadly, by members of the Indian middle class."

Under this view of the social order, according to Wiener, there is a "division between people who work with their minds and rule and people who work with their hands and are ruled"; and therefore, the children of this latter group, members of the lower castes and untouchables, should from an early age start training for their lot in life—in jobs using their hands rather than in classrooms using their minds. More sophisticated, but with the same consequences, is the theory that child labor is inevitable for societies at an early stage of their industrial development and that free market forces, left to themselves, should be relied on to bring progress over time. In a recent *Harvard Business Review* article, David L. Lindauer, professor of economics at Wellesley College and a World Bank consultant, recalled the presence of children in early American and European textile factories and added, "We know of no case where a national developed a modern manufacturing sector without going through a 'sweatshop' phase."

Actually, there are such cases in Asia itself. As Weiner points out in his book, the development policies of South Korea, Sri Lanka, and even a few parts of India (such as the state of Kerala in the south) have successfully concentrated on sending children to school rather than into industry.

Moreover, there is something weird about reaching back in history to explain that today's abusive practices in some countries are simply in sync with natural patterns of development. If there were something preordained and dictated by nature in developmental "stages," then many developing countries would reject fax machines, VCRs, jet airplanes, cell phones, and other modern wonders in order to be in historical harmony with their country's "stage" of development. This rationale depends on an illusion of the world economy as a vast machine that somehow operates on its own. Actually, it functions because of the millions of daily decisions made by persons like you and me—investors, bankers, business people, consumers, and the rest of us, all making choices.

Unfortunately, the illusion that the self-regulating machine will automatically bring an end to such abuses has a powerful hold on policymakers in and out of government. In a visit to World Bank headquarters in 1992, Horst Habenicht, who heads the ILO initiative against child labor, was shocked that the various international institutions grouped under the World Bank have a big gap in their policies: their financial lending and advice to developing countries ignore completely any consideration of how bank polices may promote or diminish child servitude. The same blind spot afflicts the officials and policies of the international trade body, the much-touted General Agreement on Tariffs and Trade (GATT), headquartered in Geneva.

At a union convention in Pittsburgh in November 1881, Samuel Gompers, later to become the first president of the American Federation of Labor, described his visit to New York cigar factories where he saw conditions that sickened him:

"I saw little children, six and seven and eight years of age, seated in the middle of a room on the floor, in all dirt and dust, stripping tobacco. Little pale-faced children, with a look of care upon their faces, toiling with their tiny hands from dawn till dark, aye, and late into the night . . . . Often they would be overcome with weariness and want of sleep and fall over upon the tobacco."

Gompers' stirring appeal for change needs to reverberate today throughout the global economy, wherever choices are made affecting child servitude. "Shame upon such crimes!" he cried. "Shame upon us if we do not raise our voices against them!"

Targeting Child Labor at Its Worst

(From the April 12 and June 25, 1999, issues of Human Rights for Workers)

AT THE ANNUAL conference of the International Labor Organization (ILO) in June 1999, more than three thousand employers, workers, and government delegates from some 150 countries unanimously adopted a new "Convention Concerning the Prohibition and Immediate Action for the Elimination of the Worst Forms of Child Labor." In defining "the worst forms" of child labor, the convention text takes specific aim at

— slavery and slaverylike practices, such as forced or compulsory labor, debt bondage, and serfdom;
— using children as prostitutes or for the production of pornography;
— using children in drug production or drug trafficking; and
— work that is "likely to jeopardize the health, safety, or morals of children."

What difference will the new convention make in the lives of the millions of boys and girls now subjected to those abusive conditions?. Bonded labor and some of the other abuses it targets are already outlawed in India and Pakistan, for example, but they flourish anyway. And the ILO itself already has numerous conventions against child labor, including two comprehensive ones adopted in

1937 and 1973, which are widely violated or ignored. The problem is that the ILO has no enforcement mechanism with teeth, nothing akin to the sanctions that the World Trade Organization applies to violations of its rules. The ILO relies solely on publicity and persuasion.

No wonder child labor is growing in the world. This expansion is confirmed by Kailash Satyarthi, an Indian who has been campaigning against child labor (or what he calls child servitude) for nearly twenty years, first in India and South Asia and now throughout the world. He originated and led the 1998 Global March against Child Labor, in which child laborers on every continent held demonstrations dramatizing what Satyarthi calls "the curse on the face of mankind."

The Global March didn't disappear with the completion of the 1998 event. Amazingly, it has built up a coalition of supporting organizations in about one hundred countries and has now grown into a vast global nongovernmental organization, with its headquarters in New Delhi and secretariat members in key countries, including the United States.

If taken seriously, the new convention may well make a difference to many girls and boys now victimized. Because of public pressure, hopefully more governments will be shamed into penalizing those who commit crimes against children and into implementing universal primary education for all children, including migrants in American commercial agriculture. Hopefully.

What gives reason for real hope is not so much the text of the convention, nor the rhetoric of the presidents and prime ministers who bestowed fulsome praises on it. No, what inspires hope is that the Global March Against Child Labor and its many allies, individually and collectively, will remain active on the world scene to ensure that the new convention will have an impact where it matters: among the millions of young children who are now at work instead of in school.

The cause is just, and it can prevail—if it gains enough support, not just in words, but in deeds.

U.S. Myopia about Agriculture

(From the June 21, 2000, issue of Human Rights for Workers)

"AGRICULTURAL WORK IS the most hazardous and grueling area of employment open to children in the United States. It is also the least protected." Thus begins a new report, *Fingers to the Bone: United States Failure to Protect Child Farmworkers,* issued in June 2000 by Human Rights Watch. The report exposes how commercial agriculture in the United States exploits hundreds of thousands of boys and girls who labor under oppressive conditions in fields, orchards, and packing sheds across the United States. Specifically:

— Every year, some 100,000 children working in U.S. agriculture suffer job-related injuries from knives, heavy equipment, and other hazards.
— Legally, growers and farm labor contractors can hire children at an age younger than in nonagricultural employment. So many ten- and eleven-year-olds hold jobs classified as agricultural.
— Since agricultural employers can legally work children for unlimited hours, twelve-hour days (and nights) are routine, as are six- and seven-day workweeks.

"The differential treatment of children in agriculture as opposed to children working in other occupations is indefensible and discriminatory," the Human Rights Watch report states. That discrimination, both de jure and de facto in character, "leads directly to deprivation of other rights, most notably the right to education and the right to health and safety."

What are the prospects for reform?

In June 1999, after vigorous lobbying by the United States, including U.S. business representatives, the UN's International Labor Organization adopted a convention "Concerning the

Prohibition and Immediate Action for the Elimination of the Worst Forms of Child Labor." Quickly ratified by the Senate, this international agreement comes into force for the United States in December 2000.

Enter Human Rights Watch with its report, a 104-page indictment. "While eager to point out abusive child labor practices in Guatemala, Brazil, Pakistan, and other developing countries, the United States is myopic when it comes to domestic abuses," the Human Rights Watch report points out. Its findings illustrate a range of child labor abuses in U.S. agriculture that violate specific provisions of the new convention—e.g., "work with dangerous machinery, equipment, and tools; work in an unhealthy environment, including exposure to hazardous substances, notably pesticides; and work for long hours, during the night, or without the possibility of returning home each day."

Thus far, the Clinton administration has claimed that the United States is in compliance with the new convention and that therefore no change in U.S. law will be required. Especially after the publication of the new Human Rights Watch report, however, the U.S. government should have a tough time sticking to that position.

But it did anyway. Because of the opposition of the agribusiness lobby, Congress has year after year failed to amend the Fair Labor Standards Act to protect children working on large commercial farms.

Under the prolonged pressure of negative publicity, the full-time employment of boys and girls under sixteen has decreased in *some* Asian factories exporting shoes and clothes to Western countries, according to an early 2008 report on corporate social responsibility by Neil Kearney, general secretary of the International Textile, Garment, and Leather Workers Federation. Nevertheless, he emphasized, child labor remains a serious problem in both the export and domestic sectors of the developing world.

CHAPTER 4

Discrimination Against Women

Globalization has brought an unprecedented number of women into the workforce, but it has done so in ways that violate the rights of millions of them. Here are some insights into their vulnerabilities in the United States and elsewhere, starting with excerpts from "Dragon in the Toy Factory," which appeared in the October 8, 1993, issue of *Commonweal*, followed by other articles published in Human Rights for Workers and in the U.S. Labor Department's *Monthly Labor Review*.

THERE'S SOMETHING STRANGE about it. In an era of unprecedented concern for universal human rights, doubts still linger about whether the basic needs of working men and women qualify as "rights."

A disaster at a toy factory on the outskirts of Bangkok ought to help erase those doubts. When a sudden fire last May [1993] destroyed a Kader-owned facility, some 188 Thai workers lost their lives because their right to a reasonably safe workplace had been grossly denied. The four-story factory was a death trap—it had no fire alarm, no sprinkler system, no fire hoses, and no fire escape; some regular exits were locked or blocked. Besides the fatalities, 379 other workers were injured.

Even as Thai officials were investigating the cause of the fire and promising to increase safety inspections of the country's many new factories, the *Economist* of London offered its historical perspective on the tragedy. "The early stages of industrialization are often rough," it explained. "Britain and America were able to afford better laws and safer workplaces as they got richer."

This kind of analysis, often deployed to put a gloss of inevitability on even the most indefensible abuses of human rights, can sound plausible to the uninformed. But in this case it clearly doesn't fit the facts. The Kader factory, owned by some of the wealthiest Asians in the region, mass-produces stuffed dolls (Bart Simpson, Cabbage Patch, and others) for highly profitable U.S. retail outlets selling to the richest consumers in the world. The enterprise has been well integrated into the global economy, one that differs radically from the historical model on which the *Economist* builds its rationale. Despite Kader's economic success, its workers have long been victimized by the company's low-wage policies. According to sources within the company, Kader has avoided paying many of its workers even Thailand's $5-a-day minimum wage by classifying them as "temporary," on renewable contracts.

The English-language Bangkok daily, the *Nation*, which does not share the detached *Economist* outlook, pointed out a significant aspect of the tragedy: "The bodies pulled out of the wreckage [at Kader] were mostly young and female. Some of them may have been underage. At least two were heavily pregnant."

The "waste" continued in Bangkok two months later when ten female workers, nine of them teenagers, died in a garment factory fire from which they could not escape because of locked doors and barred windows. Similar disastrous fires have in recent years occurred in Bangladesh, China, Hong Kong, Indonesia, and Malaysia. In Bangladesh's capital city of Dhaka, for example, three twelve-year-old girls died in a 1990 garment fire that killed twenty-five persons and injured about two hundred, the great majority of them young women.

A century ago Pope Leo XIII condemned the Western industrializing world for debasing the labor of human beings to the level of a thing, a commodity. He blamed the "callousness of employers and the greed of unrestrained competition" for the rampant exploitation of working men. Today, with competition unleashed on a global scale, working women have become the commodities of newly industrialized nations.

Goods now move farther than ever; investments do too. But personal responsibility does not. At the U.S. end, we—customers, store owners, importers, investors, and all the others—handle the finished products, concerned only about price and quality. It is easier to be callous when the people working for us are Asians on the other side of the world. After the Kader fire, a U.S. trade association quickly distanced his industry from the disaster by emphasizing that the Kader workers were *not* on the payrolls of the U.S. companies.

It's true that fewer and fewer American businesses are *directly* involved with labor in foreign countries. They own a dwindling proportion of the plants in the export industries of developing countries, even though the United States is often the largest market for their output. Instead of producing the goods themselves, U.S. companies increasingly act as distributors and marketers of products they design. Nike and Reebok, for example, have American quality control managers in Indonesia factories producing athletic shoes, but the factories, Asian-owned, work as suppliers under contract. Levi Strauss & Co., another large U.S. company that mass markets foreign-made goods, has about six hundred suppliers under contract in fifty countries around the world.

Contracting out gives the U.S. companies a number of advantages. It makes their operations highly mobile by allowing them enormous flexibility to choose among competing suppliers in a country, within a region, or even beyond and to make and unmake contracts based on the lowest cost for a certain level of quality. Suppliers compete against one another to offer labor at the lowest possible price. Local factories, squeezed by competitive pressure, cut corners. This can mean no pay for overtime work, no days off even for holidays, no sick pay, no first aid for injuries, no decent toilets, no fire escapes. The most vulnerable under this global squeeze are uncounted millions of young women at sewing machines, behind microscopes, and on assembly lines in third world factories.

Back in 1988, the Kader multinational offered a memorable example of the attitude often bred by transnational mobility. To meet the big holiday demand for Ghostbusters, Mickey Mouse dolls, and Big Hauler trains, a Kader factory in the province of China bordering Hong Kong required its young women to work fourteen hours a day, seven days a week. Troubled by such abuses, Chinese government officials objected, but as a Kader executive in Hong Kong, Andy Lee, said to a *Business Week* reporter, "We told them, this is the toy biz. If you don't allow us to do things our way, we'll close down our Chinese factories and move to Thailand."

Kader didn't have to move; it did things "our way" both in China and in Thailand.

Lambs Led to the Slaughter

(From the March 11, 1998, issue of Human Rights for Workers)

AT LEAST TWO women died, dozens more were stricken with leukemia and serious anemia, and uncounted others suffered lesser ailments from poisonous chemicals emitted by foreign shoe factories in Fujian province. Because of that outbreak two years ago, a Beijing periodical, *Chinese Women*, sent a reporter, Chen Yonghui, to Putian City, Fujian, to investigate.

Chen Yonghui found that the air in most Putian workshops she visited was so polluted that she started feeling dizzy from her first minutes there. She also found that most factories had no air purification system and that some made do with ineffective exhaust fans (which were often shut off to save electricity costs). Since the young women workers were unfamiliar with the health perils they face daily, "They really are a group of lambs led to the slaughter," the reporter wrote.

How much would it cost to clean up the toxic air? After some research, Chen Yonghui learned that an amortized investment in an air cleaning system would cost less than a half cent per pair of shoes.

Since the cost is so small when spread over total production, why don't factories install the equipment? The conventional wisdom among economists: China is "too poor" to do so. Two U.S. corporate lawyers, R. Michael Gadbaw and Michael T. Medwig, embrace that view in a contribution to a recent book (*Human Rights, Labor Rights, and International Trade*). They correctly point out that the "vast majority of workers" in the world do not enjoy basic rights, not even minimal protection against on-the-job health hazards. They then explain this situation by approvingly quoting an economist, Gary S. Fields: "The reason is simple: the economies in which they live are too poor."

Not simple, but simplistic. The young women in Putian are making shoes for economies that are not poor. The cost of making those shoes is ultimately paid by consumers in places like the United States. Pointedly, Chen Yonghui mentions that a pair of Nike shoes made in Putian sells for $120 in the United States.

During his 1999 visit to the United States, China's prime minister, Zhu Rongji, said that of the $120 U.S. retail price of a pair of athletic shoes made in China, only $2 goes to the Chinese workers who assemble them. The New York City-based National Labor Committee has calculated the direct labor cost to assemble a $90 pair of Nike sneakers to be approximately $1.20. Thus, the wages of women making sneakers amount to 2 percent of their retail price, according to Zhu, or 1.3 percent according to the National Labor Committee. I quoted that data (backed by my sources) in a letter to *Business Week*, which published it in its May 24, 1999, issue.

On a Global Treadmill

(This book review was published in the January 1990 issue of the U.S. Department of Labor's Monthly Labor Review.)

IN RECENT YEARS, millions of women in the third world have entered the paid workforce in the employ of transnational corporations and their ancillary enterprises, including contractors and subcontractors. In some Asian countries, women now form the majority of workers in a growing number of industries producing for Western markets, including the garment, electrical, appliance, semiconductor, shoe, doll, and toy industries.

A new book, *Women Workers and Global Restructuring*, edited by Kathryn Ward, an associate professor of sociology at Southern Illinois University at Carbondale, takes a rare look at the working women of the third world, as well as their counterparts in Japan and the United States. As Ward points out in the lead essay, the dominant model of economic development takes for granted that employment will automatically uplift the status of women. According to the findings reported by Ward and nine other contributors to this collection, the effect of "global reconstruction"—modern corporations in action far beyond their national borders—has been "contradictory." Their new job opportunities have liberated women to some extent while also reinforcing gender exploitation on a large scale.

Ward summarizes the results in two areas:

Subjugation by men. One important plus of paid labor for women in traditional societies is that it usually loosens the patriarchal controls of the family, but the minus is that women "move from the control of their fathers and families to industrial plants that have male managers" who perpetuate traditional male domination in new modes of exploitation.

Economic dependence. Earning money on their own often enables third world women to achieve a measure of economic independence, but the wages are generally very low—"barely at the subsistence level even by their own country's standards and up to less than 50 percent less than local men." Moreover, when women try to protect their interests through unionization, they almost always meet strong opposition from employers as well as their governments. In fact, their economic plight is so pressing that many women work triple shifts—they hold down a factory job, perform traditional child care and household functions, and also engage in activities in the so-called informal sector, such as small-scale retail trade and home production of goods under a subcontract. "A third shift has been added because of economic necessity and for survival," Ward explains.

One of the revealing insights of this book is that the global economy relies not just on a modernized formal sector but also on a large informal sector and its armies of women who struggle under nineteenth-century working conditions. The distinctly "informal" characteristics of that sector are that its activities are generally not recorded in most official statistics and that its workers, almost always women (and sometimes children), go uncounted and unprotected by even the most minimal labor standards. The workers eke out an existence "at the bottom of a subcontracting pyramid controlled by men" (to quote Ward again).

Ward defines global restructuring as "the emergence of the global assembly line in which research and management are controlled by the core or developed countries while the assembly line work is relegated to the semiperiphery or periphery nations that occupy less privileged positions in the global economy." Although the book covers three nations at the "periphery" (Colombia, Indonesia, and Mexico) and three at the "semiperiphery" (Greece, Ireland, and Taiwan), it also examines the status of women workers in two countries at the core. Both the chapter on Japan, which describes the little recognized contribution of female industrial workers to that country's "economic miracle," and the chapter on California's Silicon Valley, which describes the low status of third world immigrant workers employed in the microelectronic industry, show how gender discrimination and patriarchal-style control prevail even at the developed "core."

The contributors to this volume (nine sociologists and one economist) optimistically cite a number of examples of how poor working women across the world have protested against the exploitation they endure. True, these women are not the docile creatures portrayed by gender stereotypes; they have the ingenuity to utilize diverse tactics in their sporadic resistance to oppression. But the odds against them are enormous. As their subjugated status is documented here, it seems extremely unlikely that they, acting on their own, will be able to achieve the liberation that they have the right to expect from participation in the otherwise thriving global economy.

Sexual Harassment in Normal, Illinois

(From the April 11, 1996, issue of Human Rights for Workers)

"THIS CASE IS going to show that sexual harassment in the workplace is bad for the [company's] bottom line." That was how Paul Igasaki, the vice chairman of the U.S. government's Equal Employment Opportunity Commission (EEOC), described a class action lawsuit that the U.S. government filed in federal court April 9, 1996, against a U.S. subsidiary of Mitsubishi Motors Corporation. It may be the largest sexual harassment case in the nation's history, with monetary damages potentially reaching a total of $150,000,000.

In a pattern of abuse going back to at least 1990, women at Mitsubishi's plant in Normal, Illinois, were called "sluts, whores, and bitches, and other names which I cannot repeat," Igasaki said. They had to endure "groping, grabbing, and touching," and they found their names affixed to workplace drawings of genitals, breasts, and various sex acts, according to the commission's investigation. Some women, it was also charged, were pressured into sexual relations as a condition of employment.

"This case should have a significant impact beyond the parties," Igasaki said, "and should send the strong message that sexual harassment in the workplace, whether in office suites or on the assembly line floor, will not be tolerated, especially on the outrageous scale that we see here."

A spokesperson for Mitsubishi Motor Manufacturing of America rejected the charges. "Discrimination of any kind will never be, and has never been, tolerated at this plant," Gary Shultz, a company vice president, said.

The lawsuit comes at a time when some in the U.S. Congress are challenging the employment commission's very existence. The commission's latest initiative against sexual harassment provides ammunition that both supporters and opponents of the agency will try to use to buttress their positions. Hopefully, the controversy will throw some light not just on the domestic but also on the global dimensions of the harassment problem.

It is thanks to federal legislation, the U.S. Civil Rights Act of 1964, under which the EEOC gets its authority, that employers in the United States are now, as never before, sensitized to their legal and moral obligation to combat sexual harassment. But it is important to remember that the operations of Mitsubishi (or Motorola or IBM or Boeing or Gap) do not encounter similar legal constraints in Japan or China or Singapore or Bangladesh. Sexual harassment lawsuits impose a potential bottom-line cost on businesses in the United States that they do not face in their operations in Asia and elsewhere abroad.

Some critics claim, partly because of their concern about competitive pressures, that the EEOC is imposing an unfair burden on employers in the United States. It is ridiculous, however, to argue, as some do, that the United States must, for competitive reasons, lower its standards to those of other countries. Yet even many people who accept the need for decent standards in the United States are blind to the obligation that the huge U.S. involvement in the global marketplace imposes on U.S. international policies, governmental and corporate.

When it comes to the rights of working men and women, international commerce today is still at a primitive stage: lawless and amoral. Almost anything goes. The rationale is that world trade, unfettered by any rules on worker rights, automatically leads to a better life for the working women and men whose products we buy and stock in our homes, garages, stores, offices, and vacation sites.

When it comes to trade across state boundaries within the United States, most Americans these days reject such thinking as out of touch with modern reality. Yet American officials accept and diligently defend that rationale for trade across national boundaries, even glorifying it as "free trade." Sooner or later, this policy will be seen as morally reprehensible. Meanwhile, it is being perpetuated and promoted in the offices of multinational corporations, at meetings of international agencies such as the World Trade Organization, and in other forums where officials have the leverage (and the responsibility) to determine policy in an equitable manner.

What is the moral difference between "groping, grabbing, and touching" women making cars for us in Normal, Illinois, and doing that (and worse) to women making toys and dolls for us in Shenzhen, China?

A year later, Mitsubishi Motor Manufacturing of America reached a settlement resolving all claims in the EEOC lawsuit filed on behalf of the three hundred women who had been subjected to a pattern of harassment at its Illinois auto plant. The company agreed to pay the aggrieved employees and former employees a total of $34,000,000 and to continue a recently established "zero tolerance" policy against sexual harassment, plus training and monitoring to enforce it. According to a June 11, 1998, EEOC press release, Mitsubishi's agreement was voluntary; but it came as the commission was preparing to go to trial on the lawsuit that it had filed in April 1996.

Taking on Wal-Mart, Against the Odds

(From the July 15, 2004, issue of Human Rights for Workers)

SHE IS THE lead plaintiff in *Betty Dukes v. Wal-Mart Stores*, which is by far the largest workplace-bias lawsuit in history. Betty Dukes, a fifty-four-year-old greeter at a Wal-Mart store in California, became an instant celebrity after a federal judge ruled on June 22, 2004, that her lawsuit could go to trial as a class action embracing up to 1,600,000 past and present female employees of Wal-Mart in the United States.

Filed by Ms. Dukes and five other Wal-Mart women, the suit presented detailed statistics showing the following:

- women working in Wal-Mart stores are paid less than men in every region,
- pay disparities exist in most job categories,
- the salary gap widens over time even for men and women hired for the same jobs at the same time,
- women take longer to be promoted to management positions, and
- the higher one looks in the Wal-Mart organization, the lower the percentage of women.

A TV reporter asked Ms. Dukes why, rather than stay in such an environment, she didn't just quit. Because, she replied, she liked working at Wal-Mart, but she wanted the company to treat her and her colleagues fairly. Quitting, she reasoned, wouldn't accomplish that.

The suit, filed three years ago, prompted Wal-Mart to make some changes even before the U.S. District Court in San Francisco certified it as a class action. One change is a new job classification and pay system that, according to company officials, is intended to ensure fairness in pay and promotions. More changes will most likely follow, whether the company decides to settle out of court or let the case come to trial.

"Up to now," explained Brad Seligman, executive director of the Impact Fund, a nonprofit organization that is the lead counsel for the women, "Wal-Mart has never faced a trial like this. Lawsuits by individual women had no more effect than a pinprick. Now, however, [through class action] the playing field has been leveled. Wal-Mart will face the combined power of 1,600,000 women in court."

Note that this pursuit of justice by Betty Dukes and her colleagues affects only Wal-Mart in the United States. But what about the many more women who work for Wal-Mart and its contractors elsewhere in the world, especially in China? As Peter S. Goodman and Philip P. Pan write in "Chinese Workers Pay for Wal-Mart's Low Prices" on page 1 of the February 8, 2004, issue of the *New York Times,* "The Communist Party government [of the People's Republic] has become perhaps the greatest facilitator of capitalist production, beckoning multinationals with tax-free zones and harsh punishment for anyone with designs on organizing a labor movement."

Wal-Mart employs nineteen thousand women and men in thirty-eight supercenters and other retail outlets in China. It has an even larger presence as a mass buyer of made-in-China merchandise exported to its five thousand stores in nine countries, including 3,586 in the United States. More than 80 percent of the six thousand foreign factories that supply Wal-Mart with goods are in China.

The number of women and men who work for those Chinese contractors and subcontractors far outnumber Wal-Mart's "associates" in China (as it calls workers on its own payroll). The company issues no statistics on those who do this outsourced work, but you can get a rough idea of the size of this labor force from the staggering volume of goods its workers produce for Wal-Mart to export from China to the United States, Mexico, and a few other countries: $10,000,000,000 in 2001; $12,000,000,000 in 2002; and an estimated $15,000,000,000 in 2003, according to company figures announced in November [2003].

Whom can the Chinese counterparts of Betty Dukes turn to in China? Nowhere. Not to the courts. And of course not to the Communist Party/government-run All-China Federation of Trade Unions (ACFTU), which has no units in Wal-Mart although they are legally supposed to be established even in foreign-owned businesses. (Wal-Mart does not deal with unions anywhere in the world, a company spokesman told *People's Daily* in October 2003.)

In his June 2004 ruling, U.S. District Court judge Martin Jenkins noted that the class-action ruling comes in the year that marks the fiftieth anniversary of the Supreme Court's antischool segregation decision in *Brown v. Board of Education.* "This anniversary," he wrote, "serves as a reminder of the importance of the courts in addressing the denial of equal treatment under the law whenever and by whomever it occurs." Judge Jenkins's decision also serves as a reminder that a huge number of women in China working for American consumers have no way to assure their equal treatment under the law. How long will this outrage endure?

> The *Betty Dukes* case has yet to come to trial and may not for a while, if ever. Wal-Mart has it tied up in California courts, and if it loses its appeals there, is likely to take it all the way to the Supreme Court. A separate lawsuit, filed in 2005 by workers in China and four other countries against Wal-Mart for violations of its own code of conducf, was dismissed by a California judge in 2007 and is now under appeal.
>
> Under government pressure in China, Wal-Mart agreed in 2006 to allow its retail workers there to join the official government union but continued to oppose unions in the United States and to fight the class-action lawsuit filed against it by women workers here.

CHAPTER 5

The Anti-sweatshop Movement

Thank the Lord for the college students, many of them just freshmen and sophomores, who teach their elders lessons in global ethics. The antisweatshop protests of those youngsters, initiated in the 1990s, is part of a global movement to respect the rights of working men and women in an era of rapid and tumultuous globalization. I described the origins and early days of that movement in the article below, which appeared in the October 24, 1998, issue of *America* magazine under the title "High-Priced Shoes, Low-Cost Labor." Because sweatshops remain a scandalously large presence in the global economy, part of the antisweatshop movement is experimenting with a new way to eliminate them.

THEY WERE ONLY EIGHTEEN out of an undergraduate population of six thousand, but a year ago, under the banner of Students Against Sweatshops, they launched a campaign that targeted a lucrative commercial enterprise of Duke University. The eighteen held no campus sit-ins or demonstrations. Their most confrontational act was to have some 350 collegians e-mail the president of Duke letters of support for the campaign. This March, after a winter of negotiations, they joined university officials in celebrating

---

victory—Duke's adoption of a comprehensive code of conduct against sweatshops. The code covers the seven hundred licensees that manufacture and market the athletic shirts, caps, jackets, gym bags, and other products emblazoned with the Duke name or logo.

For the most part, Duke's code contains requirements common in dozens of codes now dotting the corporate landscape: no child labor (under the age of fourteen), no prison labor, no bonded labor, no corporal punishment, no sexual harassment, and no excessively long workweeks (beyond sixty hours). It surpasses most codes, however, in requiring compliance through unimpeded inspections by independent monitors. Its most far-reaching and unusual requirement is that licensees must disclose the names and locations of factories making items bearing a Duke symbol. That "sunshine" provision was a key demand of the Students Against Sweatshops from the very start.

Its leader, Tico Amaury Almeida, twenty, a junior whose Cuban-born aunt worked in a garment factory, was a summer intern last year at the Union of Needletrades, Industrial, and Textile Employees in New York City. Upon his return to the campus, he founded the antisweatshop group with the help of ten or so fellow students. Now Duke University officials themselves are taking up the cause and promoting it beyond Durham. Says Jim Wilkerson, director of trademark licensing at Duke and the main university official responsible for the new code, "We need a universal code that is applied across the collegiate industry."

The code breakthrough at Duke is just one episode in an international social drama of the 1990s: the struggle to gain respect for the rights of working men and women in an era of globalization. The drama's cast of characters is enormous. The media gives top billing to big names—to institutions like Duke, to personalities like Kathie Lee Gifford—but pay scant attention to the roles of people like Tico Almeida, the Duke student leader, and Jim Wilkerson, the Duke executive. Despite the lack of name recognition, they are not bit players.

The significance of these actors is hard to comprehend unless you follow their work closely as I have over the years. The players include men and women such as these three:

Rosaline Costa, a former nun who works for the Commission for Justice and Peace of the Catholic Bishops' Conference of Bangladesh. More than a decade ago, she started protesting and publicizing the plight of women in Bangladesh's garment industry. Today, thanks in part to her pioneering work, the country's 1,200,000 garment workers, mostly women, have an independent union of their own, led mostly by women.

Apo Leong, a researcher and organizer of twenty-five years' experience in Hong Kong, where he directs the Asian Monitor Resource Center in ferreting out information on what's really happening to China's workers. He traveled to Washington in March to publicize the latest findings of his center and two other Hong Kong organizations, the Christian Industrial Committee and the China Labor Bulletin.

Jeff Ballinger, director of Press for Change, which he runs out of a small office in Washington, D.C., and his home [then] in New Jersey. While working for the AFL-CIO in Indonesia years ago, he learned firsthand about the problems of women workers making brand-name athletic shoes for export. His one-man campaign, centering on factories producing for Nike, has mushroomed. It is now also being carried on by dozens of nongovernmental organizations in the United States and beyond, especially in Australia, Canada, Holland, Hong Kong, and the United Kingdom.

Costa, Leong, and Ballinger have all had their fifteen seconds of sound-bite fame highlighting their roles as sources and analysts rather than as catalysts. That focus misses much. It ignores a wider reality: the growing network of like-minded individuals and grassroots organizations now active on every continent. Their emerging social movement has dimensions, actual and potential, that even the participants hardly fathom. Diversified and yet unified in spirit, decentralized yet internationalized, the movement is without a name, without a membership roll, without central leadership, and without a headquarters, held together only by common ideals and global strands of faxes, e-mail, and Web sites, plus occasional international conferences.

Credit (or blame) globalization. It expands more than markets: it expands human perspectives and concerns. Women and men making export goods in Mexico, Malaysia, and Madagascar, newly aware of ways to protect their rights, organize real unions where before none existed. Academics and journalists start investigating the causes of worker unrest in faraway lands by talking directly with workers. Shoppers in suburban supermarkets become conscious of how they, personally, are connected with distant developments. As the 1997 Human Rights Watch report put it, "Because the goods purchased in one country may be produced by victims of repression in another, the very act of consumption can be seen as complicity in that repression unless steps are taken to ensure that manufacturing is free of labor rights abuses . . . . Many consumers [want] to avoid personal complicity in human rights abuse."

Businesses worry about such complicity too. TV footage about a brand-name product made in sweatshops doesn't help the corporate image. Of course, sweatshops generally are owned and operated by foreign contractors, not by the home corporation, but that's an excuse no longer tenable, especially since industry leaders such as Nike and Liz Claiborne have, in principle, accepted responsibility for what their contractors do. Hence, the trend, starting in the early 1990s, toward corporate codes of conduct to cover the labor practices of their myriad foreign firms under contract to make garments, shoes, toys, and other goods for U.S. consumers.

But too few corporations have adopted adequate codes. And even corporations with good codes often have poor or inadequate enforcement. In short, the codes did not become a quick fix. They did become a guide that worker activists abroad used to measure the gap between promises and performance.

After a barrage of embarrassing publicity about sweatshops even in the United States, the secretary of labor at the time, Robert Reich, saw an opening for an industrywide initiative. He persuaded President Clinton to appoint a task force—formally called the Apparel Industry Partnership, with leaders from business, labor, human rights, religious, and consumer organizations—to eradicate sweatshops from the garment and shoe industries. That partnership finished designing a model code in April 1997, but it is still grappling with the herculean task of how to enforce it, especially in China.

Meanwhile, unions and human rights groups have kept up the heat through their own monitoring of the far-flung factories where millions of Asians and Latin Americans toil for us. Last spring, one such group, the Hong Kong-based Committee for Asian Women, drew on Chinese sources for an assessment of how women workers are faring in unnamed factories in China's booming coastal provinces. "For most of [the women]," the committee said, "life is nothing but a nightmare." For young women who migrate from inland provinces to seek a better life, "just what does it mean working in shoe, toy, and electronics factories where [toxic] glues and solvents are commonly used? A gas chamber."

Nowadays, more and more field investigations identify offending factories by name. No name comes up more frequently than Nike, for whom some 450,000 foreign workers manufacture shoe and athletic equipment. An April ESPN broadcast, for example, featured videotape of the health hazards faced by young women gluing together Nike sneakers in Vietnam. "The criticism is making us a better company," Tom Clarke, Nike president and chief operating officer, commented on camera. And Nike has also said, with remarkable frankness, that it cannot fully implement its own code by itself and that it needs the help of governments and international organizations. In a statement on [and since removed from] one of its Web sites, Nike says that "workers should have the opportunity to form unions and negotiate with management on a collective basis," thereby reconfirming two commitments in its code. But that's impossible in some countries, Nike adds (without naming China, Indonesia, and Vietnam). Consequently, it advocates an international "process" to put pressure on the "intransigent" in a concerted way involving industry, governments, and unions.

Is this a ploy by Nike to pass the buck? Maybe. But Nike makes an important point, one that its statement fails to buttress. By themselves, codes of conduct cannot cure the evils they are designed to address. The codes are voluntary, dependent on the consciences of signatories. They form a useful but insufficient instrument to cope with the globalized system of exploiting the world's most vulnerable workers. That rapidly exploding system is so far-reaching, so well entrenched, and so enormously profitable that reforming it is a formidable challenge. But not impossible if pursued in concert.

This is frontier territory. That holds true also for many facets of globalization but especially for the challenge of how to cope with victimization of ordinary workers in the huge new international marketplace. This challenge has been partially addressed in the United Nations family by the International Labor Organization, but under sharp limitations in jurisdiction and orientation that stem from the ILO's founding in the pre-UN and nonglobalized world of 1919. Modern-day labor issues need to be addressed in consultation and cooperation with post-World War II international organizations—above all, with the World Trade Organization.

The WTO and the ILO are neighbors, both with headquarters in Geneva. Their relations have not been very neighborly. Within twenty-four hours after being invited to give a talk at a historic WTO ministerial conference held in Singapore in December 1996, the ILO's director general, Michel Hansenne, was abruptly disinvited. Officials of some Asian governments wanted no talk, and no talking, about the controversial subject that is Hansenne's occupational specialty: international labor standards. Still, the trade ministers and other senior officials, hailing from some 120-odd countries, couldn't sweep the issue under the rug. For much of a week, they argued about a key proposal of the United

States and a few other delegations that a WTO working party be set up to explore how to safeguard worker rights in today's global economy.

The proposal got nowhere, but the ministers at Singapore did adopt an ambiguous compromise. "We renew our commitment to the observance of internationally recognized labor standards," the ministers declared in a written statement. But they quickly added that the ILO "is the competent body to set and deal with those standards." Translation: stop bothering *us* with this stuff.

Still, making the most of slim pickings, the International Confederation of Free Trade Unions (ICFTU), whose representatives lobbied the Singapore meeting, called the outcome "a small but significant step forward in our drive to bring a human face to the process of globalization." With affiliates in 141 countries and territories representing 125,000,000 working men and women, the ICFTU in recent years has become a major nongovernmental player on the world scene. Its longtime goal to engage the WTO has been reinvigorated of late by much stronger support from unions in Asia, Africa, and Latin America. As a result, more than ever before, the major division on this issue is not North vs. South. The fiercest opposition comes not from developing countries but from the *governments* of some developing countries, supported by employer organizations in industrialized countries.

Whatever the intentions at Singapore, the issue is not buried. It got a strong boost from President Clinton in a little-publicized address prior to the WTO Ministerial conference in Geneva in Geneva May 18-20 [1998]. He urged international policymakers to do more to make sure that "spirited economic competition among nations never becomes a race to the bottom—in environmental protections, consumer protections, or labor standards." Toward that end, he endorsed the proposal long resisted by the WTO—that the WTO work together with the ILO "to make certain that open trade does lift living standards and respects the core labor standards that are essential not only to worker rights but to human rights." He specifically urged the two organizations to convene a high-level meeting to launch such cooperation.

Thus, a joint ILO-WTO approach no longer sounds as radical as it used to. In a presentation to a mid-April conference at the Institute of International Economics in Washington, Kimberly Ann Elliott, a research fellow at the Institute, urged the WTO to appoint a "study committee" on labor standards. "It would be," she said, "both economically efficient and politically wise for the WTO to take some action in the short run against the most egregious violations of labor standards."

What about "protectionism"? Richard Freeman, professor of economics at Harvard, calls it a red herring to charge that protectionism motivates the drive for international labor rights. "Union support for labor standards," he writes, "represents a principled commitment to improving the situation for workers around the world."

That commitment goes back a long way. In fact, it is just one hundred years ago that Samuel Gompers, president of the American Federation of Labor, told delegates to the December 1898 AFL convention in Kansas City, Missouri: "We should endeavor by every means within our power to cultivate fraternal feeling and interest in the welfare of the wage earners of all countries, to aid and encourage every movement calculated to materially, morally, and socially improve the conditions of the workers, *no matter where they may be located*" (my emphasis).

No one should be surprised by the current controversy over protecting worker rights, any more than by controversies that rage over global rules in other areas, such as protecting foreign investment through an international treaty. Historically, Americans found no noncontroversial way of adjusting to the transition from a coalition of sovereign states (the United States as a plural noun) into a nation-state (United States singular) with national rules on countless matters, including decent labor standards. Today too we have no easily agreed-upon ways of coping with a much more rapidly changing world. The danger lies not in debate but in suppressing it or trying to lock it up in just one institution.

The cry for global solidarity sends a powerful message to world policymakers. Failure to heed it risks a perilous backlash: an upsurge in protectionism, exaggerated nationalism, and paranoia about international bureaucracies.

Congress and the White House did not heed the warning in the concluding paragraph of this 1998 article. As a result, a backlash against globalization has increased, as reported in the following article in my May 6, 2008, posting on my Weblog. (my emphasis)

Backlash Against Globalization

(From a May 6, 2008, posting on my Weblog, Human Rights for Workers)

"IN GENERAL, DO you think that free trade agreements like NAFTA [the North American Free Trade Agreement], and the policies of the World Trade Organization, have been a good thing or a bad thing for the United States?"

Bad thing was the answer of 48 percent of Americans in a poll conducted at the end of April [2008]. *Good thing* was the answer of 35 percent. In the ten years since that question was first asked, support for global trade policies has never been weaker.

A bipartisan negative attitude on trade seems to be emerging. Half (50 percent) of Democrats rated current trade policy as bad in the April poll. So did 40 percent of Republicans and 52 percent of Independents.

These results, released May 1 by the Pew Research Center, are more bad news for and about globalization. It should be another warning to present and future U.S policymakers on trade that the status quo won't do and that just tinkering with it won't do either.

Meanwhile, the antisweatshop movement among students remains very much alive. United Students Against Sweatshops (USAS), which celebrated its tenth anniversary as a national organization in 2008, has student affiliates in more than two hundred colleges, universities, and high schools, each agitating in its own way for a "sweat-free campus" and for a "sweat-free world." To get those goals implemented, they rely on a separate national organization, the Worker Rights Consortium (WRC), which USAS founded in 1999 and which currently has the administrations of 181 college and universities as affiliates. The WRC's competitor, the Fair Labor Association, founded in 1999 at the Clinton administration's urging, has 206 colleges and universities as members. In contrast to the WRC, the FLA includes Nike and other corporations as active members.

The antisweatshop goals are disappointingly far from being achieved, however, because too few factories are living up to codes of conduct; and some important ones that adopted them found that it was impossible to operate successfully in the fiercely competitive global economy. So USAS/WRC have worked on a new approach that doesn't rely only on codes of conduct but concentrates on doing business on a sustained basis with factories selected for proven performance in respecting worker rights. That approach, still experimental, has been endorsed in principle by forty major colleges and universities.

CHAPTER 6

Why Pick on Bangladesh?

On two research assignments to Bangladesh, I conducted dozens of interviews with government officials, employers, union leaders, and others, including child workers, to assess the situation of workers in the country's booming garment industry. The evidence I collected was overwhelming: Bangladesh was violating basic worker rights and, thus, not qualified for special U.S. trade benefits—the U.S. tariff reductions it was receiving as a concession under an international program called the Generalized System of Preferences or GSP for short. As a result, in June 1990, the AFL-CIO for the first time filed a petition asking the U.S. Trade Representative to withhold GSP privileges from Bangladesh because of violations of its own labor laws as well as internationally recognized labor standards.

Here are the introductory and concluding sections of the petition. They address the objection, "Why pick on such a poor country?"

BANGLADESH, ONE OF the poorest countries in the world, has many desperate needs. None of its needs surpasses those of the country's impoverished workers—men, women, and children—whose elementary rights are flagrantly violated. Unless the government of Bangladesh takes serious steps toward respecting those rights, the country deserves to lose its GSP privileges.

Because of its serious and widespread labor abuses, Bangladesh obviously fails the worker rights test that developing countries must meet to qualify for the GSP privileges under the Trade and Tariff Act of 1984. The argument against invoking the sanctions of U.S. law is that Bangladesh is a basket case, a country so immersed in poverty that it ought not be judged by the usual standards.

That argument is based on false assumptions about U.S. law and about Bangladesh. The 1984 law does not require poor countries to achieve the standards of highly industrialized nations. In fact, it does not set down absolute standards of any sort. Rather, its objectives are modest—it seeks to prod developing countries toward "taking steps to afford internationally recognized workers' right to workers in the country (including any designated zone in that country)." In other words, no matter how poor a country, it should seek to make some progress in respecting the rights of its workers.

Is the condition of Bangladesh so utterly hopeless that it really cannot meet that minimal requirement? Absolutely not.

On the contrary, to make such a judgment about a poor country is to condemn it to remain on a treadmill of poverty and injustice. That is true as much for Bangladesh as it is for Poland or Romania.

Massive infusion of foreign aid has not enabled Bangladesh to get off the poverty treadmill. In fact, according to a Bangladeshi economist, Dr. Rehman Sobhan, former director of the Bangladesh Institute of Development Studies, foreign aid has served to reinforce the status quo and to militate against social change. (He developed this point in his book, *The Crisis of External Dependence*, published by the University Press Ltd., Bangladesh. In a 1990 interview with me, he assessed Bangladesh's economic stagnation as getting worse because of the way foreign aid is distributed. "What else can you expect," he said, "when you put large sums of money into the hands of a little group of people in the hope that it promotes the growth of the economy's private sector?")

The hope now is that the expansion of export-oriented industry will spur economic growth in Bangladesh through the creation of new jobs. Sobhan criticizes the assumption that increased employment necessarily reduces poverty. The effect of employment on an economy depends less on the *quantity* than on the *quality* of jobs being created. Do the jobs pay below-subsistence wages (as is true of most new employment in Bangladesh)? True, a job at below-subsistence pay does make a contribution at the household level where families are struggling for survival. But the contribution of such jobs to economic growth on the national accounts level is highly marginal. (This argument is drawn in part from ideas expressed by Dr. Sobhan in the 1990 interview with me in Dhaka.)

Although the above paragraphs briefly challenge some assumptions mistakenly believed to have a foundation in economics, the case we make in this paper rests not on economics but on the human rights of workers outlined in provisions of the 1984 trade act. The most shocking abuses involve young children, many of whom work in factories for sixty hours or more a week, but those transgressions are really part of a much larger pattern. Although Bangladesh has ratified both ILO conventions 87 and 98, which guarantee the basic rights of workers, it has fostered the kind of labor market where almost anything goes.

> The petition goes on to document gross violations of worker rights in six categories: freedom of association, the right to organize and bargain collectively, child labor, below-subsistence wages, excessive working hours, and occupational safety hazards. The petition then ends with the conclusion below.

The portrayal herein of Bangladesh's worker rights situation is grim. Our analysis is not exaggerated, and may even be understated, since Bangladesh offers bountiful evidence of human exploitation as evidenced by the following excerpt from a April 17, 1988, *New York Times* article [by Seth Mydans] with a Dhaka dateline:

Redwan Ahmed, the owner of Saleha Garments Ltd., said women are essential to his industry. Bred to subservience, he said, they will work for as little as $13 a month and accept harsh conditions and long hours without complaint. "If I appoint 400 men workers, they immediately start making union politics," he said. "Not the women." And with the low salaries they are willing to accept, he said, "You get more workers with less investment."

Roushan Janan, a scholar who has researched the new phenomenon of women workers, said factory owners sometimes lock their doors to keep women at their places for overtime work. She said the women often have too little schooling to compute the wages due them and are frequently shortchanged.

The August 1989 "Overseas Business Report" of the U.S. Embassy in Dhaka has this enlightening paragraph on labor costs in Bangladesh:

> Throughout the country, wages are low—$1 to $2 per day—making per capita annual income, about $185, among the lowest in the world. Some industrial workers make almost $2 per day, but the majority receives much less . . . . In practice, women receive half the remuneration of men, and children, several million of whom are the labor force, receive even less.

Unfortunately, in the absence of some counterpressure, the victimization of the most vulnerable—especially women and children—will continue in Bangladesh and will probably expand as international traders seize the opportunity to get more and more out of their investments.

We are not seeking to shut off Bangladesh from the global economy. We *are* seeking to have the U.S. government prod Bangladesh to respect elementary worker rights without which the workers of Bangladesh will never share the benefits of the global economy.

The U.S. Trade and Tariff Act of 1984 provides a tool for such prodding. For the sake of the millions of impoverished working women, children, and men, it should be used.

> The U.S. Trade Representative did not use that tool in 1990, nor in subsequent years despite a series of petitions filed by the AFL-CIO and the International Labor Rights Fund documenting continued serious violations of the rights of Bangladesh's working people. In each case, the Bangladesh government, with the help of a Washington law firm, submitted lengthy testimony claiming that it was "taking steps" to observe the required labor standards; and the U.S. government, in a very loose interpretation of the facts, accepted that claim as true. So serious worker rights abuses continued in Bangladesh as illustrated in the following article.

Greed Kills, and Greed Pays

(From the May 4, 2005, issue of Human Rights for Workers)

AGONIZED CRIES FOR help stopped after two days and nights. It took eight more days for rescuers to stop searching for bodies from under the storey-high piles of rubble that once was a seven-storey building. Even a week later, nobody knew for sure how many garment workers—women, men, and children—died when the whole structure suddenly collapsed. Estimates ran from sixty-one to over one hundred dead and many more injured.

The disaster happened during the April 11 night shift of a garment factory in a swampy area twenty miles from Dhaka in Bangladesh. Some three hundred to four hundred workers were busy filling rush orders for European retailers when the big building started vibrating enough to cause cracks in its support columns. Production continued for several hours until everything and everybody went tumbling down together in a gigantic crash.

Tragedy in its garment factories is nothing new for Bangladesh, but this one still hit hard. Demands grew for the arrest of the building and factory owners. Angry garment worker activists confronted the head of the Bangladesh Garment Manufacturers and Exporters Association (BGMEA). Women leaders of several human rights organizations demonstrated in front of the BGMEA headquarters. Impoverished relatives burying the dead couldn't help worrying about whether they could ever collect the unpaid wages of the victims. And newspapers scorched the employers and the government.

"Thousands of workers in Bangladesh put their lives and limbs on the line every day on the factory floors," the English-language *Daily Star* wrote on April 25. "It is the collusive arrangement of government agencies and the factory owners, who cut cost at the expense of safety of the workers that is the cause of so many deaths and injuries in this [garment] sector."

Without absolving the government and employers of Bangladesh, Neil Kearney, who leads the global union of garment workers, said, "The real villains are the European retailers who have sourced from that factory for years." In an address to a trade union convention in Spain on April 26, he named some of the European companies that he deemed guilty of negligence (Carrefour of France, the Cotton Group of Belgium, Karstadt Quelle of Germany, and Zara, part of the Spanish fashion distributor Inditex) and added, "Brands and retailers are the ones driving the industry today. They search the world for the cheapest source of supply, they ignore blatant labor abuses, and they pay prices that bolster exploitation."

Kearney was describing more than the bad practices of the garment industry. Those practices flow logically from something more basic, an idea with an invidious hold on many modern minds. He was describing the free competition that afflicts today's global economy—that is, competition freed of normal human values.

In its April 25 editorial, the *Daily Star* also wrote, "The casualty figures of factory accidents in the last decade would put any person with a conscience to shame." But who believes that conscience, or shame, should have any place in our current system of international trade and investment?

Even as people in Bangladesh were coping with the latest garment factory disaster, a Bangladeshi delegation was in Washington seeking passage of a law granting a tax break for the country's exports to the United States: duty-free entry into the United States for all its products. The delegation, which included representatives of the BGMEA, emphasized that without this concession from the United States the "poor women" in the garment industry, some 1,500,000 in all, would lose their jobs to competition from China.

Annisul Huq, BGMEA president, makes the same plea on his Web site: "Our greatest concern is for the women workforce who would be devastated if the RMG [ready-made garment] sector suffers." (No word on the devastation caused to women and men by factory collapses and fires.)

Upon learning of the Washington visit, I sent BGMEA President Huq an e-mail query: "Does the BGMEA support making that duty-free privilege conditional on Bangladesh's agreeing to respect the right of its working men and women to safe working places?" I then quoted from a May Day editorial of Dhaka's *Daily Star*: "This year [May Day] will be observed across the globe, including Bangladesh, with a fresh vow to institutionalize worker rights," and I followed with this question: "Now we have a timely opportunity to institutionalize those rights in a trade bill now under consideration."

True to character, the BGMEA did not seize that opportunity.

The United Nations Development Program's 2007 human development indicators for 177 countries ranked Bangladesh 137th, between Ghana and Nepal.

CHAPTER 7

Assessing China

The People's Republic of China is booming. Its GDP keeps growing. Shanghai keeps adding more and more skyscrapers. Foreign investment keeps multiplying. Yet however impressive these growth figures may be, what do they mean for the ordinary people of China? What do they mean for the development of democracy and civil society in China? In testimony in Washington, D.C., on December 9, 2002, at an open forum session of the Congressional-Executive Commission on China, I offered a different standard for evaluating the political and economic health of China. Then, in an article published in *Freedom Review*, I described my participation in a demonstration while Hong Kong was still a British colony.

MORE THAN TWELVE years ago I attended a conference on democracy sponsored by the National Endowment for Democracy and hosted in the House foreign affairs committee room, just down the road from here. It was an exciting time. Among other historic events, Solidarity had been legalized in Poland just a few weeks earlier, and so it was natural that the leadoff speaker was someone from Poland—Jacek Kuroń, a leading advisor to the Solidarity movement.

As the conference program pointed out, Kuroń was the person "most responsible for developing the strategy of building civil society" in Poland.

I was greatly impressed with the conceptual framework of Kuroń's remarks—his outline of the essential characteristics of totalitarianism. Drawing on his own personal experience in the struggle against a repressive regime, Kuroń identified "a monopoly of organization" as the key element of totalitarianism. This monopoly, he said, "is so total that if its citizens gather freely and discuss freely a matter as simple as roof repairs on a block of flats [or condominium apartments], this constitutes a challenge to the central authority." The second most important characteristic of a totalitarian state, Kuroń said, "is a monopoly on information, meaning that every printed word—not to mention the electronic media—is centrally steered by central authority." As a practical matter, he quickly added, this model is an ideal that cannot be implemented in all its fullness.

Kuroń's model of totalitarianism is a useful tool for making a serious assessment of any country at any time, and it is especially useful for making judgments about one particular country, the People's Republic of China, at this particular time. A powerful country daily becoming ever more powerful, China is in the midst of historic change, dramatized by a double transition—first, to a new generation of leaders at the top of the country's party/state command structure, and second, to a new global role in the international political economy as a leading member of the World Trade Organization.

Chairman Mao went a long way toward imposing the totalitarian ideal on China, and caused unbelievable horrors before his successors changed course. Unfortunately, although well short of the Mao-era extremes, the essential characteristics of totalitarianism survive in modern China. The regime still tenaciously holds on to its monopolies of organization and of information—even as it "opens up" in significant ways. But as a practical matter, Beijing has made selective exceptions to its implementation of the totalitarian model. Let me briefly describe one exception that fascinates me.

Consider the thriving existence of an organization called the American Chamber of Commerce in the People's Republic of China. It is headquartered in Beijing, but its influence reaches beyond the capital city. Its membership comprises more than 1,550 persons representing more than 750 companies, small and large, with operations throughout China. It is a "forum" for exchanging information inside and outside its own ranks, even with China government officials at various levels. That information covers a lot of ground. Its annual White Paper, a comprehensive survey (in English and Chinese) of the "climate" for American business in China, provides exhaustive details on both the positive and the negative features of that climate. Its analysis of labor conditions, for example, praises "positive developments . . . benefitting both international and domestic business" but also contains many complaints, such as that "labor costs in China remain higher than those of many Asian countries, and are rising steadily . . . [without a] corresponding improvement in the competitiveness of the Chinese labor market." The full text of the White Paper is available on the chamber's Web site.

Among the chamber's other activities are the following:

- Publishing a business magazine, AmCham's *China Briefs*, ten times a year. It reaches a readership estimated at five thousand, including not only 1,500 business executives but also Chinese and U.S. government officials, foreign diplomats, and directors of other chambers of commerce in the Asia-Pacific region.
- Monitoring and publicizing China's compliance with its World Trade Organization (WTO) accession agreements. Its WTO Implementation Report, released this fall, praises China's "serious commitment to meeting its WTO obligation," but it also expresses "many specific concerns . . . [about] some areas where China may not yet be in full compliance with WTO commitments." The chamber will continue this monitoring and is planning to issue an annual public report for the rest of China's five-year WTO implementation period.

There you have some details (culled from *http://www.amcham-china.org*) on an enclave of nontotalitarianism in China. In fact, that enclave offers a nontotalitarian model of how freedom of organization and freedom of information can be exercised in China, if permitted by the government. It also outlines the kinds of openness that China must attain to free itself fully from the shackles of totalitarianism.

In singling out AmCham-China, I am of course not objecting to the fact that American business people, like the business people of many other foreign countries, have successfully organized themselves and are actively pursuing their interests in a collective fashion, even to the point of lobbying the government of China. It's just that their freedoms so glaringly contrast with how thoroughly, often brutally, China denies these same freedoms to its own citizens, including its working men and women in factories, farms, and offices. This policy has a historical antecedent, nowadays in universal disrepute, called colonialism, a system whose central failing was to grant foreigners greater rights than a country's own people. It eventually inspired revolutions. Will the neocolonialism of the twenty-first century do likewise?

In an article he published in Hong Kong in 1994, just before he was again jailed, China's famed human rights advocate, Wei Jingsheng, protested against the discriminatory policy of granting foreigners various rights, privileges, and preferences denied to China's own people. "The citizens of this country will not put up with such unfair treatment for long," he warned. "We know from history that at times of great social change, unfair phenomena can easily change to the opposite extreme. That is, while it is the Chinese citizens who are treated unfairly, in the future it may be the foreigner."

Marching for Freedom

A short Hong Kong stopover that I made in early 1994 happened to coincide with a large demonstration protesting the government of China's sentencing of a Hong Kong journalist working in Beijing. Joining in the march to Beijing's consulate, I sensed how much the people valued freedom of expression. This article about

my participation in the event was printed in the July-August 1994
issue of *Freedom Review*, published by Freedom House.

THERE I WAS, a non-Asian marching down the streets of Hong Kong in a demonstration with two thousand Chinese men and women and delighted to be among them. I never quite got the hang of singing "Solidarity Forever" in Chinese, but I gradually mimicked a couple of the group's Chinese chants, which I later learned called for nothing more controversial than freedom of the press in China.

A quarter hour into the march a man at my side handed me his cardboard sign, either because he thought I had earned the right to carry it or because he was becoming weary. I never did learn what the Chinese characters of the sign meant, but the many identical ones all around somehow reassured me.

Although my feet were dragging during much of the hour-long march, I kept going largely because of the English-language song favored by the marchers, "We Shall Overcome." It pumped adrenalin into my system. My throat helped its message reverberate through the cavernous streets of Hong Kong's main business section and finally in front of the headquarters building of the New China News Agency, Beijing's de facto provincial office. There the police permitted us to stage a noisy sit-down.

It was purely by chance that my visit to Hong Kong in mid-April [1994] occurred when a people's court in Beijing issued a final ruling that provoked the protest demonstration in which I participated. The court upheld a lower court's sentence of a journalist for a Hong Kong daily, Xi Yang, to twelve years in prison. Xi Yang's misfortune was to be too energetic a reporter for someone still a national of China. He had upset China's officials with a byline article based on economic information not yet released to the China's public. The harsh punishment inflicted on him in a secret trial—and the fifteen-year prison term for his source—stirred public opinion in Hong Kong as had no event since the brutal suppression of the 1989 pro-democracy protests in Beijing.

A friend of mine who heads the Hong Kong Confederation of Trade Unions, Lee Cheuk Yan, had invited me to attend the

Sunday afternoon rally that preceded the protest march. I took the subway from my hotel in Kowloon to the rally point on Hong Kong Island. When I arrived, Lee was already on the speaker's platform addressing a large crowd, leading the chants ("Free Yi Yang") and the singing, which included "We Shall Overcome," as well as "Solidarity Forever" in Chinese. The whole atmosphere inspired me to tag along as the march began.

I had to admire the risk taken by the Hong Kong demonstrators. In China, such conduct would land them in prison or a labor camp, criminals guilty of "counterrevolutionary" activities. Even in Hong Kong they face an insecure future as Beijing's 1997 takeover comes closer and closer and as pressures on the British governor of Hong Kong, Chris Patten, become more and more intense. (Because Patten wanted to let more of Hong Kong's 6,000,000 citizens vote for the local parliament, Beijing has called him a serpent, a deceiver, and a whore.) Along the march, many cameras recorded our every move, with some photographers coming in close for portraits. How much of that videotape and film was destined for the dossiers of Beijing's security police?

Beijing's representatives often warn Hong Kong in plain Chinese: *China is watching.* Poor Xi Yang. The secret police in China had watched Xi so closely that they apparently wanted him to know that he was under surveillance. But he didn't heed the warnings. So Beijing decided to target Xi Yang not so much to punish him as an individual but mainly to teach a lesson or two—a lesson for the media "to turn watchdogs into lapdogs," as a Hong Kong newspaper columnist put it. But also a lesson for others who ignore or might be tempted to ignore Beijing's rigid rules.

According to a report in Hong Kong's leading English-language daily, the *South China Morning Post*, Xi Yang's punishment delivered a message that "frightens" even Hong Kong lawyers, accountants, and other professionals who do regular business in China. A stock analyst shared his fears about his work collecting economic information in China: "Would that constitute stealing state secrets or spying?" In the past, it would not. Now it well might.

—

Under the circumstances, it was surprising that so many people in Hong Kong joined in a public march demanding Xi Yang's freedom. Give credit to the advanced state of Hong Kong's "civil society"—advanced, certainly, compared to China. Most of the marchers were not isolated individuals but leaders and members of a network of private organizations concerned about the future of Hong Kong.

Hong Kong is still a colony, but its governors, operating under the rule of law and monitored by an independent judiciary as well as by a democratic parliament in London, have permitted the establishment of independent nongovernmental organizations, including trade unions, alongside a free press. Moreover, in defiance of Beijing, Hong Kong has so far permitted a founder of China's first free trade union, Han Dongfang, to live and work there in enforced exile, awaiting the day when Beijing permits him to return home.

In short, despite certain restrictions built into colonial law, despite a powerful business elite sympathetic to Beijing's ways and critical of Governor Patten's, Hong Kong is a Southeast Asian island of freedom standing in especially sharp contrast to the People's Republic of China. The big difference is not in impressive skyscrapers or in bustling urban centers (China has them) nor in welcoming foreign investors and traders (China now does that too, and feverishly) nor even in the role of legislative bodies (Hong Kong's legislative council, now largely appointed by the British, has little more power than the National People's Congress in China).

No, the big difference is that Hong Kong, in spite of its shortcomings, is still blessed with the underpinnings necessary for democracy: the rule of law, freedom of association, and freedom of the press. But for how long? My comarchers were demonstrating not just for Xi Yang's freedom but for their own.

In the aftermath of the Xi Yang case, even the *Far Eastern Economic Review*, whose pages usually pulsate with lyrical optimism about reforms in China, suddenly sang a different tune. The magazine's editorial titled "Truth and Consequences" characterized China as "sometimes totalitarian, sometimes authoritarian, always unpredictable," and went on to explain:

"Everybody knows that the Communist Party's authority always takes precedence over any rule of law. The upshot is that no one in China—not just journalists—can ever be sure his own luck will not some day run out."

Every minute in China somebody's luck runs out. One day in May the luck of three labor activists ran out in China's Shenzhen Special Economic Zone, which adjoins Hong Kong. According to an AP report out of Beijing (citing a "Chinese source who spoke on condition of anonymity for fear of arrest"), police arrested three men—one factory worker and two college students—for distributing copies of a mimeographed newsletter urging workers in sweatshop factories to join unions. The newsletter was sharply critical of both the government and foreign employers for the spread of labor abuses in Shenzhen. In a November 1993 catastrophe described in the newsletter, eighty-four women, mostly young women, died in a fire that engulfed a foreign-owned factory producing toys for export.

Drawing on such examples, the newsletter said it was time for China's workers to organize to protect their rights, rather than rely on the government: "Rights will not be bestowed on us but are something we must struggle for. If we unite, we will become a powerful force."

An impossible dream? Maybe. Maybe not.

In Hong Kong, in China along the Pearl River, and beyond, a David and Goliath struggle is being played out. The biblical metaphor understates the uneven odds. Communist China today towers as a powerful force strengthened by many friends in many nations. How many real friends does Hong Kong have?

China released Xi Yang on parole after he had served about three years of his prison term. Amnesty International welcomed his early release but pointed out that he should not have been jailed in the first place and that the laws under which he was sentenced were still being used to keep journalists and others (including Xi Yang's source) in prison.

CHAPTER 8

Trading in Bias

After prolonged immersion in international trade issues, I wrote this article, "Worker Rights and Free Trade," which appeared in the September-October 1994 issue of *Freedom Review*, then published by Freedom House. In the early 1990s, movements such as that of Students Against Sweatshops and Business For Social Responsibility had yet to become forces to be reckoned with. Still, even then, President Bill Clinton made the basic case for adding a worker rights dimension to international trade agreements, although he and his administration did not follow through with the effort needed to implement it.

BORING. BOR-RING. THAT'S my reaction whenever I examine books containing the arcane rules of international trade.

I have a key rulebook for world trade next to me on my desk. It's a document of 497 pages, not including an appendix of twenty-six thousand pages. It weighs a little over two pounds, nine ounces (weighed it myself). The title gives you an idea of how exciting it is: "Final Act Embodying the Results of the Uruguay Round of Multilateral Trade Negotiations (Version of 15 December 1993)." It compiles everything agreed upon in world trade talks that started in 1986 and finished in early 1994 in Uruguay (hence Uruguay

Round) under a huge international umbrella called the General Agreement on Tariffs and Trade, or GATT for short.

But this hefty new international accord is far from boring to business people and others with hard cash at stake. Consider a new subject covered in this rulebook—the protection of intellectual property rights.

Illegal copying of audiotapes, videotapes, compact disks, motion pictures, books, and other "intellectual property" on a mass production basis deprived U.S. copyright owners alone of an estimated $8,000,000,000 in lost royalties in 1993. The Uruguay Accord, for the first time, sets up an international system of sanctions to combat such high-tech piracy and counterfeiting of copyrights, patents, trademarks, industrial designs, trade secrets, and other forms of intellectual property. So this fat rulebook should soon help out Bill Gates of Microsoft, for example, who's been losing millions each year to software pirates in Mexico and elsewhere.

The agreement on intellectual property is just one of the Uruguay Round's twenty-eight sets of complex new rules backed up with enforcement powers. They cover a wide range of special interests—subsidies, tariffs, dumping, import licensing, government procurement, civil aircraft, trade in services, and so on. The Uruguay Round rules in turn build on many other rules adopted in seven previous international trade talks held since 1947 under the auspices of GATT.

GATT—the series of eight agreements—now "represents the closest thing to a uniform commercial code for world trade," as a Heritage Foundation report aptly described it. Enforcement of that code will be in the hands of the new World Trade Organization, which is to begin operations in early 1995, with an elevated status putting the WTO "on the same footing as the IMF [International Monetary Fund] and the World Bank," according to a GATT briefing paper.

From the above summary of the multitudinous new trade rules and the strong new multilateral trade institution, it's obvious that free trade does not mean that people are free to carry on international business in whatever way they please. No, they must follow vast sets of regulations laid down in GATT and enforced by the WTO and its "contracting parties" (governments), which at the start numbered 124 countries.

Clearly, the expanding global economy cannot function without some kind of rules.

But what kind? Should they be limited to a commercial code—i.e., only to rules covering business interests? Yes, say traditional trade specialists, who are mostly lawyers or economists. Or should they be expanded to cover worker and environmental interests? Although the traditionalists say no, the Clinton Administration in 1994 said yes.

Shocking many, the Administration that year decided that the WTO must broaden its outlook. Clinton personally broke the news at a press conference in Brussels after conferring with leaders of the European Union (until recently known as the European Community). Since the United States is by far the world's largest trading nation, it was not odd for its president to express strong views about trade policy. What was unusual was that he would be taking the initiative on an issue unpopular with trade specialists. He argued that it is time for global economic policies to take into account "the well-being of workers." In making his case, he linked that controversial issue with one that in recent years has become less controversial, environmental protection.

Clinton's remarks got almost no coverage in the U.S. media and are worth quoting at some length to provide the rationale for his initiative. The heart of his case was this: "As we bring others into the orbit of global trade—people who can benefit from the investment and trading opportunities we offer—we must ensure that their policies benefit the interest of their workers and our common interest in enhancing environmental protection throughout the world."

Clinton developed his case after a skeptical reporter said, with mounting unemployment in Europe and Japan, "Now is no time to be unduly concerned about worker rights or the environment." Clinton acknowledged that "every wealthy country in the world is having great difficulty creating jobs and raising incomes." The existence of "some common elements to this malady," he said, required a common search for solutions on a global basis. In regard to worker rights, he said:

- "First of all, if in order to create jobs we have to give up all the [social] supports that we have worked hard for, over decades, for working families, then we may wind up paying the same political price and social price. That is, we do not want to see the collapse of the middle class in Europe or in the United States.
- "Secondly, the issue of worker rights and the issue of the environment should be seen from our perspective as a global one . . . . If we're going to open our borders and trade more and invest more with developing nations, we want to know that their working people will receive some of the benefits and a fair share of the benefits of this trade and investment."

The mid-April 1994 meeting in Marrakesh, at which the ministers representing 104 governments signed the Uruguay "Final Act," could have been an occasion to put worker rights on the WTO agenda as a priority item. Partly because of vigorous opposition of governments representing some developing countries, however, the "Marrakesh declaration" adopted on April 15 ignored the issue. In a last-minute compromise, it was separately announced that "the relationship between the trading system and internationally recognized labor standards" would be among nine or ten new subjects to be raised for "examination" by a WTO preparatory committee. However, the ministers formally established only a new Committee on Trade and Environment, making it a "priority in the WTO." It was a breakthrough in the environmental area for exploring the kind of linkage that the United States wants discussed in the worker rights area.

U.S. trade representative Mickey Kantor and other top officials have since reaffirmed the U.S. objective on worker rights: "to advance the observance of internationally recognized labor standards among trading countries, and thereby to ensure that exploitation of workers does not distort international competition." The U.S. Omnibus Trade and Competitiveness Act of 1988 listed those standards as "freedom of association, freedom to organize and bargain collectively, freedom from forced or compulsory labor, a minimum age for the employment of children, and [minimum] conditions of work." These five standards reflect the core worker rights promulgated by a United Nations agency, the International Labor Organization.

Nobody in U.S. officialdom put forward a specific plan to achieve that goal and implement those standards. The idea alone, even expressed in general terms, stirred up a hornet's nest of opposition from business groups and trade traditionalists in the United States and abroad. Controversy alone, however, is not an argument against change.

It had taken much controversy and a long time for the United States to adapt its social legislation to the evolution of the U.S. economy from a geographic collection of largely separate state economies to an economy national in scope. Only in the 1930s did Congress and the president put into force a series of federal labor laws recognizing that individual states could no longer cope with child labor and other problems that transcend their borders.

Today there is a growing consensus that the global economy requires addressing certain social problems that previously were left up to individual nation-states. The European Parliament in 1994, by a 187-29 vote, urged GATT to adopt a social clause—the term commonly used outside the United States for the same reform. The International Confederation of Free Trade Unions (ICFTU), long a proponent of the social clause, has mounted a vigorous campaign to get its affiliates to lobby their governments. The resulting stamp of approval by dozens of unions in Latin America, Asia, and Africa contradicts the frequent claim that this is a North vs. South issue. In opposition to the policies of its own government, for example, the Malaysian Trades Union Congress (MTUC) issued a strong statement saying:

> We want a world trading system that puts the human being at the center of economic activity. We say that if the world's companies can have common global rules [established by GATT and the WTO], then so, too, can the world's workers.

This position has some historical roots. The first governmental conference on the subject of trade and worker rights took place in Berlin in 1890, called by German chancellor Bismarck and Kaiser Wilhelm II. Their message inviting European leaders to Berlin had a distinctly modern ring: "The competition of nations in the trade of the world, and the community of interests proceeding therefrom, makes it impossible to create successful institutions for the benefit of working men of one country without entailing that country's power of competing with other countries." As it happened, the Berlin conference achieved nothing, a fate shared by many similar initiatives in subsequent years.

Now the issue has resurfaced once again, and with more support than ever before. Why?

For a long time, many leaders, especially in trade unions, looked to the International Labor Organization as the solution. But as even some of its most ardent supporters now recognize, the ILO by itself cannot cope with the challenges of the global economy. It has no enforcement powers. Its major contribution, however, has been to build a significant international consensus around a set of core labor standards meant for all nations.

Another reason why the issue arises these days is that events have shaken the notion that economic growth stimulated by increased international trade automatically solves labor problems. One day in May 1993, 188 Thai workers, mostly women in their teens and early twenties, died behind locked exits in a fire that engulfed a doll factory with no fire alarm, no sprinkler system, no firehouses, and no fire escape. They had been making Bart Simpson, Cabbage Patch, and other stuffed dolls for Western buyers. Thus Thailand now has the record for the deadliest factory fire in history, but the People's Republic of China may not be far behind. Most of the newly built factories in China's export processing zones, including those in Guangdong province, which adjoins Hong Kong, are firetraps that house workplaces on the lower floors and dormitories on the upper floors. In the first six months of the 1994, according to an official Beijing publication, seven hundred factory fires broke out in Guangdong province alone. At least seventy-six workers, almost all young women, lost their lives in the worst of those fires.

Further, instead of helping eliminate the age-old scourge of child labor, the global economy is actually promoting it. Factories in Bangladesh, Pakistan, and some other developing countries are drafting hundreds of thousands of boys and girls as young as ten and eleven into full-time jobs making clothes, shoes, carpets, dolls, soccer balls, cutlery, fireworks, surgical equipment, and other goods for American, Canadian, and European consumers. (See previous chapter, "The Crime of Child Slavery.") Senator Tom Harkin and Congressman George Brown have proposed U.S. legislation banning the import of child labor products into the U.S., but it needs the support of other nations, and the WTO, to reach its objective—the hiring of adults to replace the growing army of children now working for Western consumers in third world factories and mines.

The idea of initiating some international action to rescue children from sweatshops and to save women from cremation in factories is controversial enough, but not as controversial as another proposed reform: protecting the right of workers to organize unions and to have those unions function free of governmental and employer intervention. In their homelands, U.S., Canadian, Japanese, and European corporations may have good relations with a union; when they employ workers in a far-off country, however, they generally fight unionization tooth and nail. In Malaysia, where unions have flourished in both colonial and postcolonial times, U.S. and other foreign corporations in the electronics industry have caused a regression in worker rights. The corporate executives enjoy the right to form their own business associations, nationally and regionally, but with Malaysian government support, they have crushed the efforts of Malaysian workers in the electronics industry to exercise the same right in their own country. American chambers of commerce operate in Beijing and Shanghai, but Chinese workers are prohibited by statute and by physical force from forming associations of their own.

To please foreign investors, third world governments often outlaw unions in specially created factory areas called export processing zones or free trade zones. The law in the Dominican Republic is different. It permits the 160,000 workers in its free trade zones to form unions, and the government has given legal recognition to more than one hundred of them, but to no avail. The 420 companies in the zones, most of them American-owned or associated, simply refuse to deal with any union, except in one way: by firing any worker elected as a union representative.

Young Asian women are often accorded preferential hiring because they can be paid lower wages and because they are considered more docile than men. Marsinah, a twenty-three-year-old woman in an Indonesia watch factory, wasn't all that docile. She organized a protest because the company refused to pay the legal daily minimum wage of $1.08, and a few days later, her badly mutilated body was found in an isolated hut. At least ninety-one other workers around the world were murdered in 1993 because of union activities, according to a survey of the International Confederation of Free Trade Unions. "As the economy becomes internationalized, so does antiunion repression," said Enzo Friso, who was then the ICFTU general secretary.

Meanwhile, things are not going all that well in developed countries. "The fact is that all of the industrially advanced countries are in deep economic trouble," says Paul Krugman, professor of economics at Stanford University. In a grim analysis published in the summer 1994 issue of *Foreign Policy*, Krugman writes of the increasing gap between the haves and the have-nots: "On both sides of the Atlantic, there is now a growing sense that many people are in effect economically disenfranchised, shut out of the prosperity that one might expect in what are still wealthy societies."

At the same time, the gap between rich lands and poor lands is increasing, and so is the gap between the rich and poor within China, Thailand, and other countries tapped to produce for foreign markets. And the situation most likely will worsen. It could hardly be otherwise because the world trading system as now constituted discriminates against the interests of workers in both poor and rich countries and thereby helps widen the gulf between the rich and poor across the world.

If that analysis is hard to swallow, take note of the insights of someone widely hailed for his worldly wisdom—Singapore's Lee Kuan Yew. A special section of the September 11, 1993, issue of the *Economist* glowed with euphoria about the future of the world, but found room for Lee's prognosis for American workers:

"America's top 10% will still enjoy the highest incomes in the world. But the wages of its less-educated citizens will drop to those of workers in the developing countries with equal or higher educational standards. Telecommuting [i.e., the Internet] transfers jobs worldwide."

The widening gulf between rich and poor will not be confined to the United States, in Lee's judgment. "Globalization," he said, "will widen income differences within each society."

For a self-confessed social Darwinist like Lee, that trend is no cause for alarm. Hence both he and his government ardently oppose a worker rights dimension in the WTO. For many others, however, the trend means that something is out of kilter in the world's modernization process and that the rules for world trade cry for updating to take into account the rights of working men and women.

Among the arguments used by Lee and other defenders of the status quo, the most common is the charge that the "social clause" would be an instrument of protection, a devious device for inhibiting trade because of the fear of competition. Actually, almost any of the many existing trade rules can be misused for trade-blocking purposes. The role of the WTO and its members is to prevent that from happening.

In a real sense, a social clause is antiprotectionist because it would bolster confidence in the world trading system. Rules that actively promote the rights of business people while completely ignoring the rights of working men and women are grossly unfair, and will more and more be seen that way. If the WTO persists in such discrimination against workers, it will undermine support for open trade, and foster the very protectionism it is supposed to prevent.

In a speech on "a new vision of trade" at a 1998 Geneva ceremony commemorating the fiftieth anniversary of the WTO and its forerunner, GATT, President Bill Clinton urged the WTO to begin working together with its close neighbor in Geneva, the UN International Labor Organization. He suggested that they make sure that open trade "respects the core labor standards that are essential not only to worker rights but to human rights."

Nearly nine years went by before the WTO gave its first public sign of neighborliness toward the ILO. In February 2007, the WTO secretariat announced that it had joined with the International Labor Office (the ILO's secretariat) to produce a joint study on "Trade and Employment: Challenge for Policy Research," a 114-page review of research studies. The International Trade Union Confederation hailed the study as "an unprecedented step forward toward achieving genuine coherence in the way the world's institutions work together." But not, please note, toward genuine *policy* coherence. The study's recommendations for further research did not include a study of how the WTO's own trade and investment policies redistribute income and wealth globally from labor to capital and from the poor to the rich.

Demonizing Sanctions (Everyone Else's)

(From the August 7, 1998, issue of Human Rights for Workers)

IT'S HIGHLY FASHIONABLE these days to denounce sanctions. The title of a *Washington Post* article calls them "The Snake Oil of Diplomacy." Mobil's "public service" ads condemn them. The U.S. Chamber of Commerce and other business groups mount lobbying attacks against them. In short, sanctions are bad, bad, bad. Or so it seems.

Strangely, however, the North America Free Trade Agreement (NAFTA), much loved by business, provides for sanctions against nations that violate its rules. Same goes for the trade agreements enforced by the World Trade Organization and for bilateral commercial agreements between nations.

I still have the clipping of the February 5, 1995, *New York Times* page 1 headline that announced, "President Imposes Trade Sanctions on Chinese Goods." The threatened sanctions covered $1,000,000,000 of China's exports to the United States. Why? Because China was blatantly stealing software, movies, music, and other "intellectual property" from American business. No business voices protested against those sanctions. In fact, it was a protracted corporate campaign protesting against Chinese piracy that prompted the president to take action against China and to promise reforms.

More recently, Henry Kissinger embraced sanctions in an op-ed article urging the president to call an emergency meeting of the heads of leading industrialized nations to deal with "the Asian collapse." The very first item on their agenda, Kissinger wrote, should be "an early warning system *with sanctions* to oblige both lenders and borrowers to prevent [financial] crises and make setbacks more manageable" (my emphasis).

The fact is that sanctions are inevitable in the operation of an international economy, just as they are necessary in individual nations (imagine the carnage on highways if there were no sanction against drunk driving). Corporations love international sanctions that promote commercial interests, and they are right if a given sanction makes sense. They are abysmally wrong, however, in holding that sanctions against evils such as slave labor never make sense.

CHAPTER 9

Fading Faith in "Free Trade"

The long-held American consensus on free trade is fading. Even several economists have begun to express doubts about its virtues, as I reported in the July 5-12, 2004, issue of *America*, prior to the 2004 presidential election.

IN A PRESIDENTIAL election year that has evoked keen controversy about trade, it is especially tempting to cast opinions about the issues into pro-free trade versus anti-free trade molds. But that dichotomy obscures the real issues and muddles public discussion and decision making.

A little-noticed new poll conducted nationwide in January 2004 by the University of Maryland's Program on International Policy Alternatives (PIPA) delineates today's major trade issues and reveals the division of American opinion about them. For starters, in probing people's overall views, the PIPA poll did not ask whether they are for or against free trade; instead, it sought their opinion on the "growth of international trade," providing not two but three choices.

Of the three choices, only 18 percent of respondents took the truly "anti-free trade" position, by agreeing with the statement, "I do not support the growth of international trade because I think the costs will inevitably outweigh the benefits." The other two options both began with "I support the growth of international trade in principle," but then branched off into two different positions. Only about 20 percent approved of "the way the U.S. is going about expanding international trade." Most of the respondents, 53 percent, support the growth of trade "in principle," but were "not satisfied with the way the U.S. government is dealing with the effects of trade on American jobs, the poor in other countries, and the environment."

In short, judging from this survey, most Americans support expanding trade but favor changes in the U.S. government's actual trade-related policies. An indication of this is the approval they give to specific trade agreements. About half of those surveyed support the ten-year-old North American Free Trade Agreement and its proposed extension through the Central American Free Trade Agreement and the Free Trade Area of the Americas. But many of the respondents, both among those who approve and those who disapprove of the agreements, express concerns about whether those agreements, and U.S. policy in general, adequately reflect human rights (including worker rights). Nearly three out of four respondents held that "as we become more involved economically with another country . . . we should be more concerned about human rights in that country." Even more respondents (nine out of ten) said that U.S. corporations operating in other countries should be expected to abide by U.S. health and safety standards for workers. An overwhelming 93 percent said that international trade agreements should require minimum standards for working conditions and for environmental protection.

Public opinion alone, of course, doesn't determine public policy on trade, any more than it does on gun control or agricultural subsidies. And majority opinion, whether measured at the 53 percent level or even up to 93 percent, does not necessarily lead to sound public policy. That's so especially when prevailing government policies on trade have two strong supports:

- a firm consensus among an elite of policymakers, degree-credentialed professionals, and other leading opinion makers, including those in respected think tanks; and
- a governmental and intergovernmental structure that institutionalizes that consensus.

In the United States, which is the leading force in setting and maintaining the international trade regime, current U.S. government policies on trade has both of those necessary supports. But something startling is happening to one of them. First, the consensus on trade is no longer as firm as it used to be. Second, although the international network of trade institutions built under that consensus, from the U.S. Trade Representative on up to the World Trade Organization, is not in danger, some of its policies are being challenged as never before.

Three leading challengers have garnered wide public notice because of their standing as economists, and as economists who express themselves clearly. One is Joseph E. Stiglitz, the eminent economist who won the 2001 Nobel Prize for economics. Stiglitz argues in his latest book, *The Roaring Nineties* (Norton, 2003), that the United States has mismanaged the global economy. In a talk last November at the Carnegie Council for Ethics in International Affairs, Stiglitz expanded on this charge:

> At the end of the cold war, the United States as the sole superpower had an opportunity and a responsibility to reshape the global economic order, to try to create an international economic order based on principles like social justice . . . . But we lacked a vision. The financial and commercial sector in the United States did have a vision. They might not believe in government having an active role, except when it advanced their interest. The active role they pushed for was to gain market access . . . . As a result we got some very unbalanced trade agreements.

Stiglitz's history of concern over unbalanced (i.e., unfair) public policy spans his career both as a scholar and as a policymaker. He served as a member and later chairman of the Council of Economic Advisers during the first Clinton administration and then as chief economist and senior vice president at the World Bank. Seven years in Washington gave him an on-the-job education on how economic theories, which are supposed to advance the common good, do not necessarily do so in practice. Two important examples that Stiglitz often cites are the protection of intellectual property rights and the requirement for free movement of capital across borders.

Patents, copyrights, and other intellectual property rights do need a measure of cross-border protection, as Stiglitz recognizes. But at the behest of drug companies and over the objections of the Council of Economic Advisers during Stiglitz's tenure there, U.S. negotiators delivered overprotection. "Unlike trade liberalization, which, at least, under some idealist (and somewhat unrealistic) conditions can make everyone better off, stronger intellectual property rights typically make some better off (the drug companies) and many worse off (those who otherwise might have been able to purchase the drugs)," Stiglitz writes in *The Roaring Nineties.*

Stiglitz is especially critical of the Clinton administration for launching a major change in the international development and trade system: requiring countries to remove controls on the movement of financial capital across borders. He blames this policy, capital market liberalization, for promoting global instability in the past, notably in the East Asian crisis of the 1990s, and potentially in the future, since it makes developing countries "subject to both the rational and irrational whims of the investor community, to their irrational exuberance and pessimism," he writes in *Globalization and Its Discontents* (Norton, 2002). More recently, in a *New York Times* op-ed piece (January 6) titled "The Broken Promise of NAFTA" (the North American Free Trade Agreement), he warned against the plan to extend NAFTA's provision on capital mobility to Latin America even though "the International Monetary Fund has finally found such liberalization promotes neither growth nor stability in developing countries."

Another top-ranked economist's latest book, *In Defense of Globalization* (Oxford, 2004), also attacks key elements of the trade consensus. In this and previous books, Jagdish Bhagwati, whom Nobel Laureate Robert Solow calls "our most powerful and persuasive advocate of free trade," uses his persuasive powers against—guess what? Against two of Stiglitz's targets: intellectual property rights and the unfettered flow of capital around the world.

Although he praises multinational corporations for the good they are doing, Bhagwati, by way of significant exception, condemns their "interest-driven lobbying" that caused the World Trade Organization (WTO) to adopt harmful rules. He cites, as "a prime example," the multifaceted U.S. pressure that led to the WTO agreement on Trade-Related Aspects of Intellectual Property Rights (TRIPS, for short). "Pharmaceutical and software companies," he says, "muscled their way into the WTO and turned it into a royalty-collection agency simply because the WTO can apply trade sanctions [to violators of its rules]." Unlike the legitimate trade responsibilities given the WTO at its founding in 1994, TRIPS, in his view, was like introducing "cancer cells into a healthy body," meaning that it "distorted and deformed an important multilateral institution, turning it from its trade mission and rationale."

Bhagwati has been unrelenting in his attack on the pattern of removing restraints on cross-border capital mobility. In an essay titled "The Capital Myth," first published in *Foreign Affairs* in 1998, then expanded as the lead article in his *The Wind of the Hundred Days: How Washington Mismanaged Globalization* (MIT 2002), and now summarized in his latest book, *In Defense of Globalization,* Bhagwati argues that the unfettered flow of capital around the world is "inherently crisis-prone." He blames a "power elite a la C. Wright Mills," "a definite network of like-minded luminaries among the powerful institutions—Wall Street, the Treasury Department, the State Department, the IMF [International Monetary Fund], and the World Bank most prominent among them"—for promulgating the myth that the unfettered flow of capital is a good thing. "This powerful network . . . is unable to look much beyond the interest of Wall Street, which it equates with the good of the world." In his new book, Bhagwati expresses satisfaction that both the *Economist* and the IMF have lately lost their enthusiasm for free capital mobility, but warns that "a watchful eye over the Wall Street-Treasury complex remains a necessity."

Thus, two world-renowned economists with different perspectives on the state of today's global economy have attacked two key elements of the trade consensus still embraced by Washington (and still being pushed in current U.S. bilateral and regional trade negotiations).

Unexpectedly, the underpinning of that consensus is now under assault from another economist, Paul Craig Roberts, former assistant secretary of Treasury in the Reagan administration and a former editor of the *Wall Street Journal*. Roberts, whose long journalistic, think-tank, and governmental career was devoted to promoting free trade in thought, word, and deed, now holds that the U.S. commitment to free trade is based on a "delusion" so serious that it threatens to turn the United States into a third world economy in twenty years. He disclosed his changed view early this year in three forums: a *New York Times* op-ed piece ("Second Thoughts about Free Trade," coauthored with Senator Charles Schumer), a Brookings Institution briefing, and a *Washington Post* interview.

"We all know free trade is good for us," he told the Brookings panel. "We've all learned this. [But] we live in the delusion that what is going on is free trade. It is not free trade."

Roberts does not reject a cornerstone of most economic thought—the principle of "comparative advantage" expounded in 1817 by the British economist David Ricardo. The theory is just irrelevant, he insists; it doesn't apply today, two centuries later, in a vastly different world. Why not? Mainly because: (1) Ricardo's theory assumes that two major "factors of production"—labor and capital (factories, machinery)—can't be moved offshore, but (2) today they can be, and are being, moved on a massive scale.

"The way it's working today," he told the *Washington Post*'s Paul Blustein, "firms close facilities here, remove them to China, produce there, and send the products back here. This is not the Ricardian case for free trade." Moreover, now labor effectively moves across borders as well, with Indian radiologists examining U.S. x-rays, for example, and China's software engineers writing software codes. As a result, insists Roberts, "the case for 'free trade'—that it benefits all countries—collapses."

He predicts "tremendous dislocations, just as there were in the transformation out of feudalism to capitalism," because today's global economy enables multinational corporations, in a relentless search for lower costs and higher profits, to shift their manufacturing and service operations to populous, labor-surplus countries like China and India.

More and more American workers now see that happening, actually and potentially, to their own jobs. *Their own* jobs? People don't *own* jobs; many economists argue; only capital—in the form of investments and other property, real and intellectual—confers true ownership, the type that merits active protection under domestic and international law. So protecting worker rights internationally is called protectionism; protecting property rights is not. But to large segments of the American public that distinction is meaningless.

U.S. foreign trade and employment policies have become a central campaign issue in this year's race for the presidency. Among his ideas on those policies, Senator John Kerry says that, in his first four months in office, he would make sure that all current and proposed trade agreements have enforceable labor and environmental standards (*enforceable* being the operative word). For this measured proposal, the editors of the *New Republic* accused Kerry of descending to protectionist rhetoric. They implied that, with Senator John Edwards no longer a candidate, Kerry will most likely moderate his position. Or as other pundits put it, he will move to a place they call the center, where the trade policy elite, liberal and conservative, is alive, well, and powerful.

A presidential contest should be a time during which the nation can have a spirited and frank discussion about the changing reality of global trade and the influence of U.S. policy. Let us hope that presidential politics allows for such a discussion in 2004.

That hope did not materialize then. Two years later, when popular discontent with trade policy helped Democrats gain control of both Houses of Congress in the 2006 congressional elections, the hope took new life. Once again, the results in Congress did not live up to expectations.

CHAPTER 10

A Human Face for Globalization

In my years as a diplomat in the U.S. Foreign Service, I found that, with very few exceptions, my colleagues held a quasi-religious faith in the virtues of the free trade system. They didn't convert me, but neither did I feel competent enough to challenge their strongly held views. Only later, after leaving the Foreign Service, did I fill in the gaps of my knowledge enough to write articles such as the one below. It appeared in the November 1999 issue of the *Foreign Service Journal*, the monthly magazine of the American Foreign Service Association, under the somewhat jazzy title "Workers of the World—Globalize!" It provided human and institutional background for a historic world trade meeting coming up in Seattle at the end of 1999. As you will see, I didn't have the foggiest that the summit would be a disaster. The WTO struggled to recover from the failure. A summit at Doha, Qatar, in 2001, sought to put it back on course, but so far without success, as I wrote in an article that follows, "The WTO in Crisis," published in *Ameria*

DAYS AFTER A FORMER law school student named Dita Sari walked out of a women's penitentiary near Jakarta on July 5, 1999, she resumed the kind of life that landed her in prison three years earlier. She

---

plunged into a series of meetings, large and small, about the plight of Indonesia's workers and what to do about it. At the convention of a new group that chose her as its president, the Indonesian National Front for Labor Struggles, Dita spoke movingly about her three years behind bars.

"It is painful, it hurts to be in prison," she said. "But I know there is more pain, more hurt, outside of prison." She pledged to use her new freedom, not to go into politics as some had urged, but to help build a trade union movement that would be a voice for addressing the problems of Indonesia's working men and women.

At the age of twenty-six, diminutive and soft-spoken, Dita Sari does not look like an agitator. Yet she is a vigorous member of a new class of a human rights advocates—people in rich and poor countries alike, campaigning against sweatshops and other forms of worker exploitation in the global economy. A diverse group, the ranks of these activists include people like

- Craig Kielberger, a Canadian high school student who in 1996 founded Free the Children International, which today has chapters of teenagers in twenty countries, all dedicated to the proposition that the world's young children belong in classrooms rather than in factories and mines;
- Wendy Diaz, a garment worker from Honduras whose personal testimony at the age of fifteen to members of Congress and others, including TV celebrity Kathie Lee Gifford, led to the founding of an antisweatshop group, the Apparel Industry Partnership, with Gifford herself a member; and:
- Thuyen Nguyen, thirty-five, a Vietnamese-American businessman who through a spare-time activity he calls Vietnam Labor Watch has turned the media's spotlight on labor abuses in Vietnamese factories making athletic shoes for export.

Such activities have surged in the past four or five years. The most surprising of all began two years ago when students at Duke, Georgetown, and a few other universities protested against the sweatshop origins of the T-shirts, caps, jackets, and other products bearing their schools' names. At latest count, the year-old United Students Against Sweatshops has affiliates active in 125 U.S. and Canadian universities, most of which are starting to require factories making those products to follow decent labor standards.

Those activists and their fledgling organizations have strong allies in trade unions, both national and international. Some leaders of the United Students Against Sweatshops have been interns in the AFL-CIO's Union of Needletrades, Industrial, and Textile Employees (UNITE). Dita Sari insists that her freedom is not a gift of the Indonesian governmental but the result of strong international pressure. In a letter thanking AFL-CIO President John Sweeney for his support, she wrote, "This is a sign of the universal character of worker solidarity."

Unions, old hands at combating sweatshops in their home countries, are now actively engaged on the global level. Take the Brussels-based International Textile, Garment, and Leather Workers Federation, with affiliates in 135 countries worldwide in industries notorious for breeding sweatshops. During his eleven years as the federation's general secretary, Neil Kearney has inspected factories in 140 countries, and found sweatshops festering in most of them. NGOs like the Vietnam Labor Watch are gadflies that expose specific problems, but it is Kearney who has the status and global experience to agitate for reforms in international public policy circles, including meetings of United Nations agencies. Kearney's activism is just one facet of a worldwide campaign for worker rights under the aegis of his parent organization—the International Confederation of Free Trade Unions (ICFTU), with affiliates in 143 countries and territories embracing 124,000,000 members.

So two sets of kindred people and organizations—one fledgling and the other mature, both struggling against mighty odds—are laying the foundation of something like a global solidarity movement. That emerging movement, aided by media exposures of the downsides of globalization, has succeeded in elevating worker rights to a serious issue among global policymakers. Even the two staid institutions of Bretton Woods lineage, the World Bank and the International Monetary Fund, have begun to integrate some labor concerns into their programs and policies, with advisory help from the UN's International Labor Organization (ILO).

Yet so far, the movement's success has been highly limited where it most counts—at the ground level of factories, mines, and other workplaces. There, uncounted millions of working women and men have yet to benefit from the bounties of the global economy. The ILO's human rights conventions covering the workplace are supposed to set decent labor standards everywhere, but they have done little to prevent lawlessness from sweeping across much of the globalized labor market. Since the ILO's rules have no teeth, it seemed logical to Neil Kearney and other union leaders to seek the involvement of a powerful global agency, the World Trade Organization (WTO), whose top officer once boasted that "we are writing the constitution of a single global economy." Now pressures on the WTO to get involved have reached a new peak, including regular prodding by the Clinton administration.

President Clinton will deliver the welcoming address to the trade ministers of about 160 nations who will gather in Seattle from November 30 to December 3, 1999, for the third Ministerial Conference of the WTO. As he urged in his 1999 State of the Union Address to Congress, "We have got to put a human face on the global economy." He has also called for developing a "new vision of trade [for] a modern WTO." He did that in a major address just prior to the WTO's second ministerial conference, held in Geneva last year. Here is a key paragraph from the Geneva address:

"In order to build a trading system for the twenty-first century that honors our values and expands opportunity, we must do more to ensure that spirited economic competition among nations never becomes a race to the bottom—in environmental protections, consumer protections, or labor standards . . . . Without such a strategy, we cannot build the necessary public support for continued expansion of trade. Working people will only assume the risks of a free international market if they have confidence that the system will work."

Clinton's most concrete suggestion on labor standards was to prod the WTO to cooperate with the ILO. The two Geneva-based organizations, he said, "should work together to make certain that

---

open trade lifts living standards and respects the core labor standards that are essential not only to worker rights but to human rights."

The ICFTU, which had a delegation at Geneva, called the address "a remarkable agenda-setting speech." In a May 29, 1998, *Washington Post* column titled "Globalism with a Human Face," E. J. Dionne Jr. wrote that the Geneva address marked "a major shift in America's approach to global economics."

Well, not quite. Actually, trying to get the WTO and its predecessor, the General Agreement on Tariffs and Trade (GATT), involved in labor matters has been an on-and-off goal of U.S. trade policy since 1953. At the first WTO Ministerial, held in Singapore in 1996, the U.S. delegation was under a specific congressional mandate to seek the establishment of a "working party on worker rights," but it failed to achieve anything close to that. Although the ministers endorsed the ILO's internationally recognized labor standards, they quickly added that the International Labor Organization "is the competent body to set and deal with those standards." Translation—that's none of the WTO's concern. Then in May 1998, despite pressure from the AFL-CIO, the Clinton administration, and others to address the issue, the ministers ignored it at their second conference, this one in Geneva.

Why has this objective been so elusive? First of all, multilateral trade negotiations require whittling down a huge number of objectives proposed by member states. That's especially true now that the WTO has 134 members, each with an equal vote. The United States, which carries on more trade than any other nation in the world, always has its own full agenda, based on input from a dozen or more U.S. agencies with interests in trade policy, as well as from Congress. The wide compass of current U.S. objectives is evident in a statement circulated this summer at the WTO General Council session in Geneva by the Office of the United States Trade Representative (USTR), the White House agency that took over trade policy coordination from State in 1962.

Here are a few items culled from it: completely eliminate all export subsidies on agriculture; remove restrictions on market access in services, such as communications, power, and transport; reduce disparities on tariffs on nonagricultural goods; ensure transparency in WTO procedures to the maximum extent possible; have trade liberalization support high environmental standards; ensure that WTO members continue to exclude electronic transmissions from customs duties; add new products to the sectors already included under the WTO's Information Technology Agreement; seek an agreement on transparency in government procurement; and widen the WTO's cooperation with other international agencies (the ILO being one of the eight listed by name).

USTR also urged the WTO to launch study programs to help WTO members, including the United States, "more fully understand the implication of newer topics and to build a consensus for the future." Singled out was the need for a study program to "address trade issues (e.g., abusive child labor, the operation of export processing zones, etc.) relating to labor standards where members of the WTO would benefit from further information and analysis on this relationship and developments in the ILO."

Interestingly, confidence in the ILO has expanded in government and employer circles of late. At its 1998 conference, the ILO unanimously adopted a Declaration on Fundamental Principles and Rights at Work, thanks in part to the role that employer delegates played in developing it and mobilizing support for it. Then this June, for the first time in decades, a U.S. employer delegate voted in favor of an ILO convention, the Convention to Eliminate the Worst Forms of Child Labor.

On its Web site, the United States Council for International Business explains why it favors speedy U.S. ratification of that convention: "The USCIB believes that strengthening the ILO to deal with egregious violations of labor practices serves as an alternative to pressures on corporations to develop codes of conduct. It also should remove pressure on the U.S. government to use trade agreements (e.g., fast track, WTO) to deal with labor standards."

The ILO's newfound popularity in this arena is linked to the fact that implementing its conventions and declarations is completely voluntary for its members. Serious violations of WTO principles can have serious consequences—even fines (called compensation). Moreover, the WTO has not formally delegated exclusive jurisdiction for an area of concern to any international agency, other than the ILO.

Take intellectual property rights—meaning the very practical monetary interests of people and firms suffering multibillion dollar losses in global markets through piracy of their writings, inventions, computer programs, films, industrial designs, and other works. The basic principles regulating this (very literally) free market are the responsibility of a Geneva-based neighbor of the WTO—the World Intellectual Property Organization (WIPO). The WTO works very closely with it, aided by the WTO's own agreement, the Trade-Related Aspects of Intellectual Property Rights (TRIPS), which is backed by sanctions.

This concerted protection of property rights creates an anomaly in the case of trademarks such as those owned by Disney, says ICFTU general secretary Bill Jordan. As he puts it, the WTO "ensures that Mickey Mouse now has more rights than the workers who make toys because it covers trademarks but not labor standards." In this respect, the government of India is consistent. It opposes any WTO regulatory role in labor standards *or* in intellectual property rights.

A strong case can be made for adopting some kind of WTO agreement on trade-related aspects of international labor rights, for which a good acronym would be TRAILS. Many worker rights abuses in the global economy are indeed trade-related. To attract foreign investments in manufacturing industries dedicated to exports, governments of developing countries regularly suspend or ignore their labor laws and practices designed to protect their own citizens. In Bangladesh, special legislation deprives fifty thousand workers in two export-processing zones of rights guaranteed by the country's labor code, including the right to form unions. In China, government labor inspectors go easy on foreign-invested factories that violate China's labor regulations (against a seven-day workweek, for example) out of fear that the Taiwanese and Korean owners will shift their toy, garment and shoe production to Thailand or Vietnam.

Nonetheless, it is clear that the Seattle ministerial won't give the green light to a TRAILS agreement, however strong the case for one might be. Many developing countries oppose even a WTO dialogue with the ILO—a suggestion Clinton made sixteen months ago—as the first step down a slippery slope to dangerous results. They just plain don't like any kind of trade/labor linkage.

Two widely expressed arguments against a serious linkage—meaning incentives for compliance and penalties for noncompliance—are that it would be a tool for protectionism and an intrusion on national sovereignty. The governments of Egypt, India, Malaysia and Singapore are among the leading WTO members voicing both objections. Among economists, nobody airs warnings on both counts more frequently and vigorously than Jagdish Bhagwati, a prominent scholar of international economics at Colombia. In his defense of free trade, he argues strongly that worker rights is none of the WTO's business, but adds that neither is the protection of investor rights as projected in a possible multilateral agreement on investments.

According to economics professor Richard B. Freeman of Harvard, union support of labor standards is not motivated by protectionism. Rather, it "represents a principled commitment to improving the situation for workers around the world and, in particular to strengthening the position of unions in developing countries." He believes that the various groups who have raised the issue "have performed a valuable service in forcing the bankers, finance ministers, trade specialists, and multinationals who dominate rule-setting for world trade to recognize that many citizens have concerns about standards that affect working people."

So will the WTO make any progress at Seattle toward addressing concerns about standards that affect working people?

No, says Jerome Levinson, professor of international law at American University and research associate at the Economic Policy Institute. Based on his analysis of U.S. labor initiatives in the past two decades of regional and global trade talks, he claims that the U.S. government position on worker rights is mostly rhetorical, never pressed with the toughness that has won U.S. negotiators concessions in other areas (for example, in opening up foreign markets for American technology firms).

But perhaps the worker rights outcome at Seattle will be different. At a minimum, Seattle's atmospherics will be different, perhaps different enough to make trade history.

Like the WTO's two previous ministerial conferences in Singapore and Geneva, the one in Seattle will attract thousands of people, fitting within one of three concentric circles: (1) an inner circle, composed of trade ministers, other negotiators, advisers and staffers, all belonging to governments or to the WTO; (2) a middle circle, composed of WTO-accredited representatives of business, labor, other nongovernmental organizations and the media, with some direct contact with liaison people from the inner circle; and (3) a nongovernmental outer circle, composed largely of people and groups quite unhappy with the WTO, some of whom are eager to shut it down immediately.

Because of the size of each of these three circles, Seattle will certainly live up to its billing as the biggest trade meeting ever held in the United States. In fact, because of a mass presence in its outer circle, it will probably be the largest trade gathering ever held anywhere—and quite possibly the most tumultuous, at least on the streets.

At the 1998 conference, thousands of protesters, a few of them peasants from southern India, disturbed the tranquility of Geneva by waving banners and shouting "Make love, not trade," "Stop the WTO," and "Resist neoliberalism." Though almost all the demonstrators were peaceful, some torched cars, smashed a U.S. fast-food restaurant's windows, and sprayed graffiti on bank walls. A union staff member who was in the conference's middle circle said at the time: "They make us look like sweet reason."

The umbrella group that organized the Geneva protest, People's Global Action, will be at Seattle. So will a newer group, the Ruckus Society, which for months has been openly training hundreds of Seattle-bound activists, Americans and foreigners, in what it calls "advanced" techniques of civil disobedience. A single militant theme—mobilization against globalization—will unite dozens of NGOs with different policy goals, such as prohibiting genetically engineered food, preserving agricultural subsidies, attacking multinational corporations, and preventing the resurrection of the Multinational Agreement on Investment (MAI) that died at the

OECD in Paris last year after a worldwide Internet campaign against it. (The City Council has designated Seattle a "MAI free zone.") In addition, much more so than the Geneva protest, the one in Seattle will attract a large contingent of overseas advocacy groups, mostly from Asia, bearing personal testimony about problems for which they blame the WTO.

Another telling difference, very dicey politically, is that the Seattle protest will include hundreds—perhaps thousands—of workers from the ranks of the AFL-CIO, especially from the Longshoremen and Steelworkers' unions. Reactions of U.S. unions during and after the conference may be crucial to congressional approval of major policy decisions made in Seattle and in the new round of trade negotiations set to follow next year. Partly because of union opposition, Congress has already twice—in 1997 and 1998—turned back Clinton's request for "fast track" authority, under which Congress commits itself in advance to either pass without amendment a trade agreement as presented by the administration or to reject it within a fixed time period.

In contrast to some other events at Seattle, the agenda of labor's own preconference meetings and rallies has a positive thrust: to make both the WTO and the global economy more worker-friendly—not to demonize globalization or agitate for the abolition of the WTO. At the conference itself, the official labor representation will number at least forty people, delegated there by the international confederation in Brussels and by affiliates in more than twenty developing and developed countries around the world. Thus the labor design for Seattle is based on synergy between union representatives in the middle circle and its much larger outer circle, on the one hand, and also between key union leaders and inner-circle government members from their home countries.

Ordinarily, trade policy is b-o-r-i-n-g. Its complexity makes it largely incomprehensible, even to some reporters covering it. It does not usually produce graphic TV footage. But if only because of the expected presence of four thousand media representatives, Seattle packs greater potential for making an impression on the general public. It could well lead off network newscasts and break into the front pages beyond the *New York Times* and the *Wall Street Journal.* If it does, the impact on public opinion and public policy will depend on how the events come across. Will they be portrayed as dominated by crowds of banner-waving radicals or by people, governmental and nongovernmental, groping for ways to put a human face on the global economy?

Whatever the outcome at Seattle and however it is reported, the issue of worker rights in the international marketplace is bound to remain very much alive. Dita Sari and those in solidarity with her across the globe will make sure of it.

The Seattle summit was not boring. Neither was it successful. Conference sessions, already marked by sharp disagreements, were completely disrupted by large and riotous street demonstrations. So for its next ministerial conference in November 2001, the WTO chose an ultrasecure setting on a tiny peninsula on the Persian Gulf—the city of Doha in Qatar. After six days of discussion there, delegates adopted a six-thousand-word document as the agenda for a new round of trade negotiations—the Doha round, successor to a hoped-for Seattle round that never happened, also called the Doha Development Round. It has run into troubles of its own, as I wrote in the following article.

The WTO in Crisis

This article appeared in the January 1-8, 2007, of *America* magazine under the above title and the subtitle "Why the Trade Crisis Can Be a Blessing." One of its themes was that the collapse in trade negotiations offered policymakers time to reassess their sometimes conflicting goals. They did not seize that opportunity, at least not in 2007 or in 2008.

INTERNATIONAL TRADE CONTINUES. So do trade negotiations, but with a very big exception. Those under the global umbrella of the World Trade Organization have collapsed. At the end of July [2006] the WTO's ruling general council agreed to an indefinite suspension of the negotiations in the Doha Development Round launched five years ago in Doha, Qatar. "The round is dead," said Kamal Nath, India's trade and industry minister. "It is definitely somewhere between intensive care and the crematorium."

Explanations for the breakdown abound. The United States blames the European Union for failing to cut its exorbitant subsidies to agricultural interests, and the EU blames the United States for the same thing. Both are right. But the deeper explanation is that WTO leaders, paradoxically, have been trying to do both too much and much too little.

At the 2001 Doha conference, the trade ministers agreed in principle that the focus of the development round should be on the needs of developing countries. Nevertheless, they loaded the agenda with at least a dozen other major items (market access for nonagricultural products, trade and investment, and intellectual property rights, among others) and dozens of minor ones, all contentious. Subsequent summits—at Cancun in 2003, Geneva in 2004, and Hong Kong in December 2005—sought unsuccessfully to narrow the conflicting views among the organization's 149 members, especially between the developed and developing countries.

A clear example of the division between the rich and poor world was, and is, the WTO's standing agreement on Trade-Related Aspects of Intellectual Property Rights, or TRIPs, which promotes not free trade but global monopolies on patents, copyrights, industrial designs, trademarks, and other forms of intellectual property. Although global protection of property rights is necessary, TRIPs goes too far. Most notoriously, it overprotects and thereby feeds the opulence of the global pharmaceutical industry, to the point of restricting the right of developing countries to export to other developing countries the generic drugs they manufacture.

Even as the WTO has been taking on much too much, it has done far too little about deviating from the standard free trade model that it so diligently tries to implement [which leaves poor countries little flexibility to shape their own path for economic progress]. Developing countries, more united than ever, resisted that model—or "mind-set," as India's Kamal Nath called it—as unfit for the development round. The resulting gap in positions, especially on agricultural issues, led to the breakdown in negotiations.

According to the metaphor of some free trade enthusiasts, promoting trade is like riding a bicycle—you have to keep moving ahead, or else you'll tip over. Well, the WTO has tipped over. But the crisis can be a blessing. Global trade policymakers can now take the time to assess whether they have been moving in the right direction.

Here the influence of the United States as the world's economic superpower, and the world's richest market for imports, is crucial. How the U.S. government exercises that influence is guided by the policies and procedures of a key trade law, the 304-page Trade Promotion Authority Act, enacted in 2002. It not only sets U.S. trade policies and the agenda for trade negotiations. It also enhances the President's decision-making power on trade, notably by being able to speed trade agreements through Congress without normal committee hearings and without the possibility of amendments (that's why the law was originally known as Fast Track).

The law expires on June 30 this year [2007], and that too can be a blessing. It squeezed through the House at three thirty one July morning four and a half years ago by a very narrow (215-212) margin and only after painful political arm-twisting. Public opinion, never enamored by free trade as defined and implemented by both Democratic and Republican administrations, has soured further since then.

The shape of globalization depends largely on global trade and investment policy, and global trade and investment policy depends largely on the United States government. Hence the Congress and the White House will not be able to avoid taking a position on the controversial issues involved in formulating a new trade law, one more in tune with the American public.

What ought that position be? That is a multibillion-dollar question with no easy answers. Here are two studies with a few answers.

In the aftermath of the failed WTO summit in Cancun in September 2003, the secretariat of the Commonwealth countries—a loosely organized group of fifty-two countries historically linked to the United Kingdom—asked the Institute for Policy Dialogue at Columbia University to do a study of what a true "development round" would look like. The study concluded two years later that the so-called development round did not deserve its name. In the book *Fair Trade for All: How Trade Can Promote Development,* Joseph E. Stiglitz, professor of economics at Columbia, who founded and directs the Institute, and Andrew Charlton of the London School of Economics describe the findings of their research in the context of world trade policy

Most American economists and trade policymakers, as well as economics professors, have a taboo against connecting trade and fairness. As shown in poll after poll, most Americans do not share that mind-set. Precisely as economists, however, Stiglitz and Charlton make a major contribution by defying their profession's taboo. They insist that considerations of fairness—or call it equity, or social justice—belong at the heart of the international trading system and that trade agreements should be judged by whether they are fair and fairly arrived at.

That means, for example, that *"any agreement that differentially hurts developing countries more or benefits developed countries more* (say, as measured by the net gains as a percentage of GDP) *should be presumptively viewed as unfair"* (the italics are the authors'). Under the fairness standard, Stiglitz and Charlton find that the Doha round, and today's entire trading regime, is unfair—loaded against the interests of developing nations. And they call the WTO, "by process and structure, a mercantilist institution that has worked on a principle of self-interested bargaining."

Significantly, again contrary to prevailing economic doctrine, the authors hold that human rights issues legitimately belong on the WTO agenda. Among the issues they cite are government "restrictions on collective bargaining and the right to take collective action." Also, "clearly, when individuals are forced to provide labor services (e.g., when they are prisoners) or [businesses are] allowed to use child labor, costs of production may be lowered. As a global community, we do not want to provide economic incentives for such behavior. On the contrary, we want to discourage it."

Stiglitz and Charlton trace a good deal of today's trade inequities to decisions reached in 1993 at the end of the Uruguay trade round, which founded the WTO. Those decisions "reflected, in large part, the priorities of developed countries." As a result, developing countries received only a small share of the gains of that round, and they also had to accept "a remarkable range of obligations and responsibilities" that still burden them. Little wonder that, in the years since then, governments and people in poor countries became increasingly disillusioned with promised benefits that never materialized.

There is a lot of room for argument about which WTO reforms are wise and feasible, but there should be none about the basic principle for a healthy trading system: that its rules should be fair.

A second major study worth wide attention is a project of the Canada-based International Institute for Sustainable Development (IISD). It focuses on the body of international law that covers foreign investors and investment—a legal area that stirred no public controversy until the late 1990s. At that time, the twenty-nine-member Organisation for Economic Cooperation and Development (OECD) tried its expert hand at creating a binding set of international rules in this important area and failed. When the contents of the draft, called the Multilateral Agreement on Investment (MAI), became public, it triggered a public outcry from more than six hundred organizations across about seventy countries. The most telling objection was that it focused on the rights of investors and ignored their obligations.

Realizing that the multilateral route was perilous, governments then focused more on comprehensive bilateral (government to government) and regional free trade agreements that contain MAI-like provisions protecting investors. While the Doha round remains sidetracked, the bilateral negotiating route is all the more attractive for developed countries. The *Economist* in its August 5 issue explains why: "In a global trade round, the big players lock horns with each other . . . . Outside the multilateral system, however, the biggest powers are free to pick off smaller economies one by one." The president's Office of the U.S. Trade Representative has sought to take advantage of this opportunity. With two regional and eight bilateral free trade agreements already in force, it has intensified bilateral negotiations with several countries. Congressional votes on two of those new agreements, with Colombia and Peru, are scheduled for spring, and will provide an early sign of the new Congress's attitude toward renewing the president's fast-track trade authority.

Like the ill-fated MAI, investor protections in those treaties and agreements cover a large amount of ground, both in their broad definitions of foreign investment and in the generous protections given to those investments and their investors. "One-sided instruments," Luke Eric Peterson, a senior IISD staff member, calls them. "They do a great job of protecting investment (property rights, contracts, intellectual property), but do not provide protection for other human rights, nor do they place countervailing responsibilities on foreign investors."

In seeking a more balanced approach, the Institute has developed what it calls a Model International Investment Agreement for Sustainable Development. Howard Mann, a coauthor of the model, explains its chief objective: "It redirects international investment agreements away from a simple set of investment rights and government obligations to an interconnected set of rights and obligations for investors and governments alike, with additional recognition of the role of civil society and local communities in this mix. No existing agreements do that."

The IISD is making developing countries aware of the model agreement and concludes that the existing approaches "do not have a long-term future," says Mann. He adds: "One can argue about many of the details [of the model], but we believe that the fundamental principle is unassailable: it is never a good thing to have rights without obligations."

Ten years ago, the first director general of the newly founded World Trade Organization, Renato Ruggiero, declared, "We are no longer writing the rules of interaction among separate national economies. We are writing the constitution of the single global economy." A grandiose vision. It needs to be brought down to earth by a vision of a diverse global economy based on rules that are

---

106

fair and on rights that have corresponding obligations. The 110th Congress, reinforced by additional fair trade-minded senators and representatives thanks to the November elections, will have a great opportunity to do just that.

A Bill of Rights for the Global Economy

(From the February 2002 issue of Human Rights for Workers)

IN THE FINAL paragraph of my article, "The WTO in Crisis," published last month in *America,* I quoted something that the first director general of the World Trade Organization, Renato Ruggiero, said ten years ago. "We are no longer writing the rules of interaction among separate national economies," he declared. "We are writing the constitution of a single global economy."

I then characterized that statement as "grandiose." It seemed to me too ambitious a vision of what the WTO was trying to accomplish. Still, upon further reflection, I think that Ruggiero may have been on to something. He may have been pointing to a little understood truth about the modern global economy: that it is a new reality, a reality whose rules were evolving into a kind of global constitution.

He called it a "new phenomenon," according to the press release issued October 8, 1996, but he explained the term only by saying that WTO has many more developing countries as members and as representatives on its Geneva staff. But could today's global economy be a "new phenomenon" in a much more profound sense? U.S. trade statistics provide a clue. About 40 percent of the goods that cross U.S. borders are shipments between units of the same multinational corporation. In 2005 the total value of such trade—commonly called intrafirm trade—came to $1,059,000,000,000, according to the U.S. Census Bureau.

Conducted on a global scale, intrafirm trade is not just old-fashioned trade writ large since it departs radically from traditional market transactions between two unrelated parties, or so-called arm's-length trade. Instead, intrafirm trade "amounts to a substitution of these market-based transactions by internal, nonmarket transactions within the multinational firm," Wolfgang Reinicke writes in his book *Global Public Policy*.

Reinicke, economist, political scientist, and keen explorer of today's economic universe, sees globalization as a new reality—"not a mere *quantitative* intensification of an ongoing trend dating back to the 1960s [but] a fundamental *qualitative* transformation of the international system." Globalization, he points out, "is for the most part a corporate-level phenomenon":

> It entails the application of new forms of industrial organization such as flexible manufacturing, coupled with the cross-border movement of increasingly intangible capital (including finance, technology, information, and the ownership or control of assets). This spatial reorganization of corporate activity leads to the emergence of a single, integrated economic geography defined by the reach of corporate industrial networks and their financial relationships.
>
> These networks and relationships cut across multiple political geographies, challenging the operational dimension of internal sovereignty, as governments no longer have a monopoly of the legitimate power over the territory within which these private sector actors organize themselves.

So as Renato Ruggiero suggested, the world's trade ministers (wittingly or not) may have indeed been writing a de facto constitution for globalization. If that is so (I am now persuaded that it is), then it follows that the world's policymakers need to get busy and write a bill of rights that embraces more than just multinational corporations.

CHAPTER 11

Unions Work to Catch Up

Out of the blue one day in the fall of 2000, I got an e-mail from Bob Guldin, editor of the *Foreign Service Journal*, the American Foreign Service Association's monthly magazine, which a year earlier had published an article of mine on international trade issues (see chapter titled "A Human Face for Globalization"). "Hi, Bob," Guldin wrote. "I have an idea for an article that you might want to work on: how labor is dealing with globalization." Thus began a long process that finally resulted in the publication of my 2,500-word article titled "Can Labor Catch Up with Globalization?" in the July-August 2001 issue of the journal. To illustrate the human issues involved, I devoted the first third of the article to how a union in Sylacauga, Alabama, confronted globalization.

IT HAD THE EARMARKS of a David and Goliath confrontation. A small local union in the little Alabama town of Sylacauga was taking on a giant multinational based in Paris. And a twenty-eight-year-old factory worker who had never crossed the Atlantic, Keith Fulbright, was flying off to Brussels, London, and Paris, on his own vacation time, to line up European support for his union's cause.

The David from Alabama was not aiming to slay this Goliath. Keith Fulbright did go forth armed—with a French-subtitled videotape that portrayed the plight of his union through the words of a dozen rank-and-file members. One of those members explained the terms of the confrontation. "We aren't against the company," he said, "but we all like to be treated fair. I feel like the only way we can accomplish that is with the union."

That union, Local 3516, the only union in Sylacauga (pop. 15,000), was fighting for its life. A merger negotiated in Europe in 1999 pushed two plants located across the street from each other, one unionized and the other not, into the same corporation, a leading international producer of industrial materials named Imerys. Thanks to this transaction, the unionized workers became a minority of the merged workforce, now totaling four hundred workers. Imerys decided that it would no longer recognize the union, which had represented workers at the unionized plant for twenty-nine years; it argued that the union was not qualified to speak for its workers.

Fulbright's European assignment in January 2000 was to challenge that position. A skilled worker at the nonunion plant, he was joined by Joe Drexler, an experienced staffer of Local 3516's national union, the Paper, Allied-Industrial, Chemical, and Energy Workers International Union (PACE). With the help of the video, they told Belgian, British, and French labor leaders of worker support for the union and management's opposition to it. "Unions must work together," Drexler said, "to keep multinationals from destroying us." Their presentations were especially effective in France and Great Britain, where Imerys has a record of friendly cooperation with unions. At several of the company's largest plants in Britain, union stewards began wearing stickers saying, "Stop Imerys Union Busting in the U.S."

The participation of an ordinary American worker in a solidarity mission to Europe was a new twist on a technique that has worked well in the United States: bringing in rank-and-file workers from Central America to testify at college forums and congressional hearings about abuses in factories producing for U.S. consumers.

Fulbright's innovative mission was a turning point in an intensive yearlong campaign to win support for his union's cause. Two other initiatives illustrate the scope of that campaign.

In March last year, union dignitaries descended on Sylacauga to speak at a large barbecue and rally. One flew in from Brussels—Fred Higgs, the general secretary of the International Federation of Chemical, Energy, Mine and General Workers' Unions or ICEM for short, the "global union" with which PACE is affiliated. Higgs told the rally that ICEM, with 20,000,000 members worldwide, was putting its full weight behind the workers in Sylacauga. He called Imerys a "chameleon corporation" for trying in America what it would not dare attempt in Europe and promised, "We'll make it so hot for Imerys that they will be looking for a solution." In a public demonstration of solidarity, some 250 persons, with Higgs at the lead, marched a mile through Sylacauga before peacefully dispersing at the Imerys factory gates.

Then, in May last year, Drexler and European union colleagues took their story directly to the annual meeting of Imerys shareholders in Paris. Although Sylacauga was not on the agenda, it unexpectedly dominated the last half of the meeting. The shareholders heard presentations from the floor that sent a shudder through the audience, according to the Paris newspaper *Liberation*. A French-speaking ICEM representative who held the proxy of Walden Asset Management, which owns four thousand shares in Imerys on behalf of socially concerned clients, pointedly asked, "Mr. Chairman, why is your company involved in antiunion practices in the United States while at the same time your company is improving its relations with unions in Europe?" In response, Imerys CEO Patrick Kron promised that "the company would not campaign against the union."

Meanwhile, the labor movement at various levels used the power of the World Wide Web to communicate the union's message well beyond its own immediate constituency. People far and wide could read all they wanted to know (in English and French) about the Sylacauga struggle, including details of Imerys's corporate history, excerpts from a manual Imerys used to train managers on keeping the plant "union-free," and the text of a PACE-ICEM complaint filed with the U.S. State Department charging violations of the Guidelines for Multinational Enterprises adopted by the Organization for Economic Cooperation and Development (OECD).

The campaign worked. In a secret ballot election conducted by the National Labor Relations Board on June 22, 2000, the union scored a 205 to 181 victory to represent Imerys's four hundred workers in Sylacauga.

Adapting to globalization is a crucial challenge facing the labor movement around the world, from the small unions in towns like Sylacauga to global union confederations like ICEM. To remain close to their constituents, unions function largely on a geographically limited basis. Modern corporations do not; they cut a wide swath across multiple political geographies, far beyond the range of traditional union structures. To bridge that gap for the struggle in Sylacauga, unions mobilized local, national, and international resources within the labor movement itself while also pursuing an external campaign by appealing to Imerys's stockholders, the OECD, and the general public via the Web.

That pattern comprises the framework of a larger union plan to cope with globalization, not only by greatly strengthening their own internal networks across international boundaries but also by reaching outside those ranks to enlist the cooperation of nongovernmental organizations, intergovernmental agencies, and even multinational corporations. In short, the lesson for unions is that, without losing their workplace roots, they too must globalize.

Unions have not kept pace with today's vast, shifting global production system, comprising 63,000 multinational parent firms with 690,000 foreign affiliates, with thousands of cross-border mergers and acquisitions a year. "We're twenty years behind," says Kenneth S. Zinn, ICEM's North American regional coordinator. Despite that immense lag, he is optimistic about catching up. "We have no choice but to fulfill our obligations to workers and the communities where they live."

Happily, the environment for catching up has improved in recent years. The idea that working people everywhere have basic rights is becoming more widely accepted than ever, at least in principle.

More than ninety years of missionary work by the UN's International Labor Organization is finally winning some converts among the elite, including the leaders of some multinational corporations and some international agencies. Last year, UN Secretary-General Kofi Annan convinced CEOs of fifty multinational corporations to join with human rights organizations and trade unions to embrace a Global Compact in support of worker rights, including freedom of association and the effective recognition of the right to collective bargaining. And in his January 2000 swan song after three years as chief economist of the World Bank, Joseph Stiglitz delivered an address loaded with ideas considered radical for someone with his background in mainstream economics and in the top ranks of an international development organization. Stiglitiz's key point: "Labor unions and other genuine forms of popular self-organization are key to democratic economic development."

Recent activism by the labor movement and its allies is partly responsible for generating this more favorable environment for worker rights, and unions are taking advantage of it by pursuing new arrangements with new partners to meet worker needs in the global economy. The major organizations involved in this endeavor are global unions (such as ICEM), which are international associations of individual national trade unions grouped by industrial or occupational sectors. Now ten in number, the global unions, traditionally called International Trade Secretariats, have updated their technologies, hired new people, and restructured themselves to handle a large range of global issues, including world environmental policies. Their size alone (ICEM covers ten sectors) is bound to impress, and it puts them into a position to pursue labor strategies on a global scale. For example, ICEM and some other global unions are pressing individual multinationals to adopt formal "framework" agreements that (1) set the broad labor policies that cover all the corporation's workplaces, even those without a union and (2) establish procedures for regular meetings between management and union representatives.

Take the global framework agreement signed last July between ICEM and the Freudenberg Group, the German-based conglomerate that makes components for other manufacturers, particularly in the auto, engineering, and footwear industries. The agreement, covering thirty thousand people in forty-one countries, commits the corporation to respect the ILO's core labor standards in all the work sites of Freudenberg and its subsidiaries. Unlike internal codes of conduct adopted by many corporations these days, the Freudenberg-ICEM agreement is fully verifiable by the union.

"We see here our future," says Truus Erkins, a Dutch trade unionist who sits on Freudenberg's European Works Council. In the future that he foresees, the standards of European workers will be eroded by globalization if workers in the United States and elsewhere are denied the protection of a union contract. Erkins was one of the four members of the Freudenberg European Works Council who visited the United States last year to learn about labor conditions in general and specifically in Freudenberg's unionized and nonunionized facilities in the United States. A U.S. industry journal, *Rubber & Plastic News*, praised Freudenberg "for demonstrating a social conscience . . . [and] for being smart."

ICEM also negotiated a framework agreement with Statoil, the Norwegian-based oil company, in 1998. Other global unions have made similar arrangements with some employers or employer groups in the international shipping, garment, metal, and other sectors, although so far they have reached only a tiny number of the world's multinationals.

To cope with globalization, unions today are negotiating with another set of powerful players in the global economy: intergovernmental institutions. Unions have always represented workers in dealings with employers and governments; now, they have greatly expanded their efforts to represent worker interests in institutions such as the World Trade Organization, the International Monetary Fund, the World Bank, and regional multilateral banks. They are asking those institutions to follow the precedent of the OECD, in which labor, like business, has a voice through an advisory committee. Such a change would enable union representatives to influence policies and projects that affect workers' lives and their right to organize and bargain. Some knowledgeable experts, including economist Joseph Stiglitz, agree with the labor charge that the present policies of international financial institutions often undermine worker rights, especially the right to organize and bargain.

Promoting worker rights in the rules that govern the global economy has long been a major priority of the world union body, the International Confederation of Free Trade Unions, which groups national union federations like the AFL-CIO, and of global unions such as ICEM. Historically, they have successfully concentrated these efforts in the arena of the International Labor Organization, where, uniquely in the UN system, they are partners with employers and governments. But their five-decade-long, on-and-off effort to match the influence that business has in the World Trade Organization and its forerunner, the General Agreement on Tariffs and Trade, has been an utter failure.

Labor's efforts at the World Bank and at the International Monetary Fund have done a little better. During a half century of life, the World Bank and IMF—founded, funded, and controlled by governments—have operated under a vision limited by governments and the financial fraternity close to governments. Only recently have they come to grips with the role of civil society, the network of private institutions operating in the landscape between individuals and the state. The World Bank now has civil society specialists on duty in Washington and in about seventy-five of its ninety offices in the developing world. And according to information the Bank's top officials gave union leaders, the bank now does take several core ILO rights—antislavery, anti-child labor, and nondiscrimination—into account in its activities, but not freedom of association and collective bargaining.

The labor movement's strategy of seeking dialogue with major centers of global power meets resistance from inside the power centers, of course, but also from small groups on the outside that are convinced that multinational corporations and international agencies are hopelessly beyond reform. After several union leaders (including ICEM's Higgs) joined corporate CEOs in launching Kofi Annan's Global Compact, a group of human rights and environmental activists expressed a relatively mild form of this dissension. They publicly criticized the compact as a sham, a means for corporations to "wrap themselves in the flag of the United Nations to 'bluewash' their public image while at the same time avoiding significant changes to their behavior."

If labor's reform strategy fails to achieve significant changes in behavior (and not just in rhetoric) fairly soon, the present criticism, which is still isolated and subdued, will become louder, more radical, and perhaps more influential. Meanwhile, unions throughout the world are following a nonradical strategy to deal with the transformations wrought by the global economy. Will that strategy make a difference where it counts the most—in the places men and women work, both in industrialized and developing nations?

In Sylacauga, the results are mixed. In early February, seven months after the union's election victory, Imerys and the union signed a three-year collective bargaining agreement with pay increases of about three percent each year, plus improved benefits. A few weeks later, the two sides came into conflict after management unilaterally adopted two sets of personnel policies, including employee guidelines listing thirty-nine infractions that would lead to discharge or lesser penalties. A flurry of worker grievances followed, as did a complaint from the union to the National Labor Relations Board that the company wasn't playing fair because it failed to negotiate the policies.

Says Keith Fulbright, now president of the Sylacauga union, "It's a struggle. But we're getting an education in how to cope."

Labor unions still have a long way to go to catch up with globalization, but they have taken some strides forward. Their single most important step occurred in late 2006 in Vienna, Austria, when a fractured world movement united to form the International Trade Union Confederation (ITUC), headquartered in Brussels. By bringing together under its roof some 304 national trade union affiliates in 153 countries and territories, the ITUC gained a stronger voice in defending the interests of all the world's working men and women and their families.

Pursuing that mission in Washington, D.C., in December 2006, an ITUC delegation composed of representatives from thirty-five countries from all the world's regions met with top executives of the World Bank and the International Monetary Fund. Their most important achievement was an agreement whereby the $8,000,000,000 worth of infrastructure projects funded by the bank each year will be required to respect the ILO core labor standards. The same standards had earlier been applied to the bank's private lending arm, the International Finance Corporation, thanks to organized labor's lobbying.

Meanwhile, global unions such as the ICEM have continued to make global framework agreements with multinationals to guarantee respect for labor and environmental rights wherever the company operates. By late 2008, of the seventy-six such agreements in all, fourteen were with ICEM. But the French multinational Imerys was not among them. It continued union-confrontational policies in Sylacauga, Alabama, and even spread them to its plants in England.

CHAPTER 12

Global Awakening

In the spring of 2000, I had the good fortune to go on a research assignment in Southeast Asia, a region I had previously gotten to know firsthand as a U.S. Foreign Service officer and then as a staff member of the AFL-CIO Asian Institute. In Hong Kong, Jakarta, Bangkok, and Manila, over a four-week period, I talked at length with workers, union leaders, employers, government officials, staff members of international financial institutions, human rights activists, and others. Then, after completing a report for an Agency for International Development project, I wrote this article, "Global Awakening," which was published in the September 22, 2000, issue of *Commonweal* magazine under the title "Workers of the World."

THE COMPUTER-GENERATED SIGN at the door of a meeting room in the Asian Development Bank (ADB) headquarters near Manila announces: "Worker Rights: Brown Bag 12:15 p.m."

Inside, more than two dozen ADB staff members, none with a brown bag but some with sandwiches, are assembled during lunchtime. They are listening to and talking with five Filipino guests: three union leaders and two representatives of nongovernmental organizations. It is the first-ever dialogue between bank staffers and people representing working men and women from the country in which the ADB has its headquarters.

In a half-hour slide presentation, Isidro Antonio Asper, vice president of the Philippine Federation of Free Workers, focuses on how ADB policies affect ordinary people and why the bank must become more responsive to their needs. Instead of imposing loan conditions restricting increases in the legal minimum wage, for example, the ADB "should help our government understand that workers need a living wage," so that (among other reasons) child labor can be eliminated. Asper's point is later amplified by his four colleagues, all members of the Philippine branch of a new network of trade unions, nongovernmental organizations, and academics in Indonesia, Malaysia, the Philippines, and Thailand.

A bank staff member challenges Asper's assertion that the ADB imposes antilabor restrictions on some loans. But a senior bank official, Ayumi Konishi, intervenes to say that ADB has indeed imposed such restrictions, and cites a specific case in Thailand in which he was personally involved.

One of Asper's key points is that, before making major decisions—such as on privatization or deregulation—the ADB should release information about its plans and should negotiate with nongovernmental representatives of civil society about the plans' impact on people. The idea of negotiating raises eyebrows and an objection: how can unions, with only a minority of the labor force as members, claim to represent all workers? Hal Ponder, Philippine country representative of the AFL-CIO's Solidarity Center, who is sitting in on the meeting, responds with a question of his own: "If trade unions can't speak for workers, who can?"

During fifteen minutes of friendly conversation after the program ends, Konishi, the top bank official present, emphasizes that ADB could benefit from outside input, especially to "challenge our assumptions," and that it needs to engage in "dialogue on overall issues—we have not done this."

It was toward the end of a four-week research trip to Southeast Asia in the spring of 2000 that I had the opportunity to attend the session at the ADB. I couldn't but be impressed. One bank staff member, although also impressed, sent me a cautionary note later via e-mail: "Getting through the door, and being taken seriously by the ranking hierarchy, are two entirely different matters."

Still, that meeting is a sign of the times, exemplifying a global phenomenon. Although the concept of international worker rights is far from a recent creation, in the past few years it has reached the tipping point of recognition where it can now be discussed even in the hallowed halls of the ADB.

Like the distinguished seventeenth-century Frenchman in a Molière play who exclaims, "My lord, I've been talking prose for the last forty years and have never known it," some distinguished international institutions awakened, late in the twentieth century, to an everyday reality whose significance they had not grasped earlier—the role of "civil society" (all those private groups, agencies, and organizations that interact to create a society's patterns and tone). Two of those newly enlightened institutions are the Washington-based World Bank and the International Monetary Fund. Founded, funded, and controlled by governments, they both until recently limited their operations to governments and the financial fraternity close to governments. Under pressure, the two vast bureaucracies have gradually opened their offices and their minds to outsiders. The World Bank now has "civil society specialists" in about seventy-five of its ninety offices in the developing world. Regular and often intensive consultations with labor and environmental groups—national and international—are becoming frequent.

In 1995, for the first time in its history, the World Bank devoted its prestigious annual World Development Report to the working world, with an entire chapter on unions. "Free trade unions," it affirmed, "are a cornerstone of any effective system that seeks to balance the need for enterprises to remain competitive with the aspirations of workers for higher wages and better working conditions." The report then weighed the positive and negative sides of unionization, and concluded cautiously that the effect of unions can be positive or negative, depending largely on government regulation. Since then, the ADB has gradually rated unions somewhat more positively.

—

At a conference on corporate responsibility and globalization held in 1999 at the U.S. Chamber of Commerce in Washington, the Reverend Leon H. Sullivan, author of the Sullivan Principles for companies in South Africa in the apartheid era, spoke about the need for new Sullivan Principles to "help companies to put their houses in order" in the global economy. United Nations Secretary-General Kofi Annan is a convert to that cause. For almost two years, he has been promulgating a new Global Compact on human rights, labor standards, and the environment. At UN headquarters on July 26, 2000, executives of nearly fifty multinational corporations became the first business members of a new international coalition of private-sector leaders to "embrace and enact" the compact, not only in their individual corporate practices, but also in lobbying for public policies. Among other things, the compact calls on world business to uphold "freedom of association and the effective recognition of the right to collective bargaining."

Those developments at the UN, the World Bank, and several other international institutions reflect the gradual awakening of the world's elite to the fact that globalization, for all its marvels, has serious downsides. Even Thomas L. Friedman, foreign affairs columnist of the *New York Times,* who is often euphoric about globalization, recognizes that fact. In *The Lexus and the Olive Tree* (Anchor, 2000), Friedman writes that it is necessary to address the problem of sweatshops and other abuses of worker rights. For many workers around the world, he says, oppression by totalitarian states "has been replaced with oppression by the unregulated capitalists, who move their manufacturing from country to country, constantly in search of those who will work for the lowest wages and lowest standards." As a consequence, Friedman points out, "people in the developing world are increasingly focused on worker rights, jobs, the right to organize, and the right to decent working conditions."

But the challenge remains of how to have those rights implemented in an international labor market that is still largely a lawless jungle, with a globe-girdling gap between principles and practice, between rhetoric and action.

Convinced that the toothless rules of the UN's International Labor Organization no longer suffice, many unions in both developed and developing countries have long campaigned to link worker rights and trade rights in the rule-making and rule-enforcing powers of the World Trade Organization (the WTO, like the World Bank and the IMF, is not part of the UN system). That campaign, embraced by the Clinton administration, shook up the historic WTO meeting in Seattle in late 1999. Thanks in part to opposition from the governments of some developing countries, even a very modest U.S. proposal—to establish a committee to discuss the state of worker rights in the global economy—failed, but the campaign nonetheless scored a public-relations triumph. TV coverage of large and occasionally violent street demonstrations made millions of people here and around the world aware of issues that the media ordinarily consider boring.

An unforeseen consequence of the campaign aimed at the WTO has been to reinforce labor initiatives that bypass the WTO. The UN Global Compact is one. Another beneficiary has been the International Labor Organization. The ILO, never widely favored in its previous eighty-one-year history, emerged with unprecedented financial and moral support as the international organization to deal with worker rights. The U.S. Council for International Business, for example, which represents U.S. employers in the ILO's tripartite structure, now says openly that "strengthening the ILO to deal with egregious violations of labor practices . . . should . . . remove pressure on the U.S. government to use trade agreements (for example, 'fast track,' WTO) to deal with labor standards."

A great deal of the new support for the ILO has an ulterior motive: to ensure that, among international institutions, the ILO keeps the labor cause as its own property, not to be touched by the WTO or any other effective mechanism of enforcement. The maneuvering is a continuing drama, with the plot action taking place not in isolation but within a larger context—the conflict over the direction of globalization. In this raging controversy, many influential individuals and organizations have voiced their discontent with the present shape of globalization. Amid the prolonged economic tumult that first erupted in Asia in mid-1997, Robert E. Rubin, then secretary of the U.S. Treasury, called for reforming "the architecture of the international financial system." Jagdish Bhagwati, a professor of economics and a vigorous proponent of free trade and of the WTO, nevertheless criticizes the WTO's powers to enforce patents and other intellectual property rights through trade sanctions. President Bill Clinton has repeatedly pressured the WTO to adopt reforms aimed at giving it a "human face." None of them—Rubin, Bhagwati, or Clinton—fits the caricature of being antiglobalist.

The real controversy, therefore, is not over whether to reform the WTO and its sister institutions but over how to do so, and ultimately for whose benefit. There are two schools of thought on the matter. The dominant school sees the international agencies' role as guiding the evolution of a global economy according to a single capitalist model, with various minor variations. A 1996 comment of Renato Ruggiero, the WTO's first director general—"We are writing the constitution of a single global economy"—epitomizes that sweeping vision. The other school has a narrower focus. It is represented by Dani Rodrik, professor of international political economy at Harvard. He insists that capitalism is a country-by-country phenomenon, with versions that vary widely, and that trying to impose a single global capitalist model on the world is a grave error. He favors letting nations have the widest possible latitude to choose their own development paths. They should be free, for example, to regulate cross-border capital movements themselves, instead of bowing to international rules dictating the unimpeded flow of such transfers. Jagdish Bhagwati also feels strongly about this issue and has accused a largely American "power elite"—on Wall Street, in the Treasury Department, State Department, the World Bank, and the IMF—of promoting free capital mobility to pursue the self-interest of Wall Street, which that elite "equates with the good of the world."

It is simplistic, therefore, to categorize these controversies as globalism versus antiglobalism. True-blue antiglobalists—those wanting to shut down or cripple the WTO, the World Bank, the IMF, or the ADB, or all four—are few. They are scarcer still among workers. During my trip to Asia I did not find workers shouting

"Stop the world—we want to get off." Rather, workers are demanding reforms so that they can get on the globalization bandwagon and gain their share of its bounty.

Nor does antiglobalism appeal to trade unions. It goes against their nature. The raison d' être of unions is not to drive corporations out of business but to reach binding agreements with them, whether at the plant, company, industry, or national level. That spirit carries over to the international arena. There, the union goal is to get an agreement on labor rights fit for the modern world economy, not to throw a monkey wrench into it.

Just as the debates over globalization no longer center on whether global financial institutions need reform but rather on how they should be reformed, so the controversy over international worker rights is no longer about whether they need strengthening but by what means. Most mainstream economists continue to hold that the elimination of labor abuses depends on economic growth, without the intervention of governments or government-run international institutions. But that position is losing ground. A few economists have even come to see the need for a governmental role in linking trade rights with some form of worker rights. Another option, now illegal under WTO rules (except for prison-made goods), is to permit any country to ban the importation of goods made in gross violation of its own standards. Dani Rodrik favors such a procedure, but only in a limited way: for example, to comply with widely held norms of the importing country barring child labor.

The position of Joseph Stiglitz, former chairman of President Clinton's Council of Economic Advisers, now a senior fellow at the Brookings Institution, transcends both the minimalist and maximalist approaches to shaping the global economy. He has developed a strong case that "worker rights should be a central focus" of economic development. In contradiction to the neoclassical economic assumption that considers human labor as just another "factor" of production, Stiglitz has attacked a great batch of faulty economic propositions that have "served to eviscerate the rights and positions of workers." It is time, he asserts, to "begin a shift in the prevailing paradigm."

Pope John Paul II is the world's leading advocate of the same general idea. Globalization "must be managed wisely," he told a crowd of two hundred thousand on May Day 2000. *"Solidarity too must become globalized"* (italics in the Vatican text). Achieving that solidarity will require a commitment from everyone, including owners, managers, financiers, retailers, professional people, and workers, he said, because of the world's failure fully to respect human dignity and to give "due consideration [to] the universal destination of resources."

As a moral principle, the "universal destination of resources" is traditional in Catholic teaching (it is discussed in the new *Catechism* in the chapter on "Thou Shall Not Steal"), but its meaning is usually kept safely general, certainly not as specific as the teachings on sex. For the 2000 Jubilee Year, however, the pope has translated the principle into a very specific goal: canceling or reducing the huge international debt that burdens many poor nations. On May Day he renewed his call for debt relief, appealing "to the rich and developed nations, but also to people of great wealth and to those who are in a position to foster solidarity among peoples."

But globalization has built into it a larger set of powerful instruments that, for good or for ill, affect human solidarity: foreign investment and trade in goods and services. How, specifically, can wealthy nations and people, through expanded international trade and investment, do more to achieve the universal destination of resources? That question has still not been given due consideration.

In fact, we have hardly scratched the surface of the potential for human progress opened by globalization. The prevailing paradigm no longer suffices to take advantage of today's boundless opportunities. Despite increased global awareness and concern, designing and implementing a new paradigm, whether inspired by Stiglitz or John Paul II, will not be easy. It needs a huge commitment of human ingenuity and funding, along with public and private cooperation—a commitment on a scale at least equal to, say, the project to chart human DNA or to build the international space station.

CHAPTER 13

Global Insights

Among my favorite authors are two economists, Wolfgang Reinicke and Dani Rodrik, as is evident elsewhere in *Justice at Work*. Here I reprint my reviews of two books of theirs that especially impressed me: Reinicke's *Global Public Policy* and Rodrik's *The New Global Economy*. The first review appeared in the January 1999 issue of the *Monthly Labor Review* published by the Bureau of Labor Statistics of the U.S. Department of Labor; the second, in the November 1999 issue of the same magazine.

A Flawed Formula

GLOBAL PUBLIC POLICY: Governing Without Government? By Wolfgang H. Reinicke, the Brookings Institution Press, 1998, 337 pp. $42.95 ($18.95 paper).

LONG BEFORE U.S. Treasury Secretary Robert Rubin and other top policymakers from the G-7 nations began talking about a "new architecture" for global financial markets, Wolfgang H. Reinicke, an economist and political scientist specializing in international institutions, was busy devising a new model for globalization as a whole. The result is this book, written while Reinicke was a senior scholar at the Brookings Institution (he is now [in 1999] with the Corporate Strategy Group at the World Bank and remains a nonresident senior fellow with Brookings).

Reinicke's model takes into account what he describes as a "sweeping, radical transformation" in the world from economic interdependence to globalization. He draws a careful distinction between the two. Interdependence, in his analysis, refers only to a quantitative intensification of international commerce, a trend going back to the 1960s. But more recently much of the world economy has undergone a qualitative change—a transformation involving not only an explosive growth in trade and investment but also, more importantly, a vast expansion of corporations across national borders. He cites an important indicator of this development: intrafirm trade across borders in 1994 accounted for about 40 percent of total U.S. trade. "Globalization," he writes, "is for the most part a corporate-level phenomenon."

Reinicke does not deplore this corporate expansion. Rather, he sees it as a natural outcome of technological innovation, deregulation, and liberalization of cross-border economic activities, which in combination have not only permitted but even compelled companies to adopt global strategies. On the other hand, says Reinicke, corporate expansion across borders—i.e., globalization—has created a split between the world's economic and its political geography, to the point that governments can no longer fully determine public policy within their own borders. Thus, contrary to economic interdependence, which evolved around challenges to a country's external sovereignty, globalization challenges a government's internal sovereignty.

Reinicke argues that the institutions and principles that have governed the international economy since World War II are no longer adequate because they are based on economic interdependence structures, where the lines of political and economic geography were identical and sovereignty was univocal. Short of an alternative, he argues further, governments often react with approaches based on a notion of national sovereignty that is tied to the continued territorial integrity of the state. He cites two traditional ways that governments try to cope: by intervening defensively to aid domestic business (e.g., through protectionism) and by intervening offensively (e.g., through aggressive export promotion and subsidies to aid home corporations abroad). Neither is sustainable as countries retaliate.

The appropriate alternative, Reinicke writes, is to "rebundle" the diverging political and economic geographic lines by evolving toward international "networks of governance" that include not just governments and intergovernmental agencies but private-sector organizations such as corporations, consumer groups, foundations, and unions. Instead of global government, which he dismisses as utopian and undesirable (a "top-heavy, imposed construct"), he proposes a global system of "public-private partnerships" that involves delegating to nonstate actors some responsibility for writing and enforcing agreed-upon rules and standards internationally. Such partnerships would take advantage of "these [nongovernmental] actors' better information, knowledge, and understanding of increasingly complex, technology-driven, and fast-changing public policy issues" and would "generate greater acceptability and legitimacy for [global] public policy."

To illustrate the realistic basis of his proposed architecture, Reinicke devotes long chapters to three case studies covering issues in which global public policy is already gradually being developed in accordance with his model, though still in a fragmented way. These three international examples are the supervision of banking and finance, the control of money laundering, and the management of trade in dual-use (military and commercial) technology. In an analysis written before the economic turmoil in Thailand and Indonesia exploded into an international crisis, he hails financial markets as the pioneers in setting global public policy, but adds that they still have far to go: for example, in achieving coordination among competing international institutions with overlapping responsibilities in the same area.

Through public-private partnerships of some kind, global rules are being developed in areas beyond those documented in Reinicke's book. A very recent example is the new international convention against bribery, adopted by governments in the framework of the Organisation for Economic Cooperation and Development with the advice and blessing

---

of both business and labor groups. Further, global rules on worker rights are now being addressed in the International Monetary Fund and other institutions beyond the tripartite (worker-employer-government) framework of the International Labor Organization. It can be logically inferred from Reinicke's analysis that social justice issues like international labor standards would also be part of his architecture. Indeed, the scope for global public policy is potentially as broad as globalization itself

Reinicke recognizes that there are dangers to granting nonstate actors some power, along with government, to formulate and implement global rules. But he sees that as a necessary risk for averting serious chaos as globalization grows. Further, he holds that spreading these responsibilities around could foster the development of a global civil society, countering the "democracy deficit" (as it is called in Europe) that is inherent in letting unelected international bureaucracies assume larger and larger roles under globalization.

Global Public Policy has no blueprint. Its paradigm of democratic governance, Reinicke points out, needs much further work to "find new avenues, institutions, and instruments that reach beyond the current political geography of the nation-state." Exploring that territory is especially complex because the end of the twentieth century is characterized by "a coexistence of interdependence and a globalization that cuts across both countries and industrial sectors."

Reinicke's book is not an easy read, but it deserves careful study by anyone who suspects that the present world architecture needs updating and that the incumbent chief architects may not have all the answers.

Wolfgang Reinicke is now managing director of the Global Public Policy Institute, an independent think tank based in Berlin and Geneva.

The New Global Economy

The New Global Economy and Developing Countries: Making Openness Work By Dani Rodrik. Washington, Overseas Development Council, 1999. Distributed by the Johns Hopkins University Press, 167 pages, $13.95.

LIKE CLOTHES, ECONOMIC development policies are subject to changing fashions. This book analyzes today's predominant theory of development, "openness"—meaning the free market in goods, services, and capital across borders—and finds it a flawed formula for poor countries. The author, Dani Rodrik, a professor of international political economy at Harvard University's Kennedy School of Government, recognizes the benefits that can flow from openness, but contends, as the main theme of his book, that "these are only potential benefits, to be realized in full when the complementary policies and institutions are in place domestically." Besides, the free market gains claimed "by the boosters of international integration . . . are frequently inflated or downright false."

Too many governments and international institutions, he writes, are fixated on openness as an end in itself. This approach, he warns, has three basic flaws for countries in the process of integrating into the world economy:

- By itself, openness is an unreliable mechanism for generating sustained economic growth. He provides data showing that countries with rapid economic growth "typically also become more open; but the converse progression—from increased openness to faster growth—is much less apparent."
- Openness tends to widen income and wealth inequalities within both developed and developing countries.
- Openness exposes countries to periodic external shocks that can trigger domestic conflicts and political unrest. Oil crises, sudden reversals in capital flows, and other shocks "will always be part of the global landscape." Economic policies fixated on openness leaves a country especially vulnerable to such shocks.

"Hence, openness is a mixed blessing, one that needs to be nurtured if it is to be a positive force for economic development." An important strategy in making openness work, he writes, is for a country to develop its own internal "complementary policies and institutions": for example, a regulatory apparatus for capital flows, transparency for trade rules, civil and political liberties, free labor unions, noncorrupt bureaucracies, independent judiciaries, and social safety nets. He provides specifics on how such institutions and policies help developing countries cope with turbulence in the world economy and with the widening inequalities that openness often brings.

Reversing the usual development advice emphasizing growth through exports, Rodrik argues that the benefits of free trade lie on the import side—specifically, importing ideas, investment goods, capital, and institutions. He frowns on development thinking that "puts the cart before the horse by vastly overstating the role of exports." He also criticizes national policies catering to foreign investment to the point of subsidizing and otherwise favoring it over domestic investment. He backs up these and other points with case studies and extensive statistical analysis of data from the World Bank's files, the Penn World Tables, and other sources.

In making his case, Rodrik takes passing swipes at "free market religion" and "knee-jerk globalizers." But this book is not an attack on globalization or capitalism. Instead, here, as in other writings, he advocates letting countries develop their own form of national capitalism, rather than trying to impose a universal model on all. He cites the United States, Sweden, Germany, and Japan as examples of market-based economies that have important differences (for example, in their style of corporate governance, regulatory framework for product and labor markets, and extent of social insurance). In the book's final sentence, Rodrik writes, "A suitable international economic system is one that allows different styles of national capitalism to coexist with each other—not one that imposes a uniform model of economic governance."

Although Rodrik slips into undefined economic jargon from time to time, you don't need a degree in economics to get his message. Unfortunately, the book has no index.

Dani Rodrik published *One Economics, Many Recipes: Globalization, Institutions, and Economic Growth* in 2007.

CHAPTER 14

Economics with a Soul

His pioneering study in the 1970s on the "asymmetry of information" won Joseph E. Stiglitz the 2001 Nobel Prize in Economics, as recounted in my article (below) published in the December 7, 2001, issue of *Commonweal*. His further work on the asymmetry of wealth and power led him to criticize conventional development and trade policies, to the point of turning against the North American Free Trade Agreement (NAFTA), which he had once promoted as a member of the Clinton administration.

AT GALA CEREMONIES in Stockholm on December 10, 2001, Joseph E. Stiglitz, professor of economics at Columbia, will receive the highest honor of his profession—the Nobel Prize in Economics awarded by the Royal Swedish Academy of Sciences. Stiglitz shares the prize with two other American economists, George A. Akerlof of the University of California at Berkeley and A. Michael Spence of Stanford, for contributions they made back in the 1970s. The Nobel committee chose them for having "laid the foundation for a general theory of markets with asymmetric information," meaning the unbalanced condition in which "actors on one side of the market have much better information than those on the other." In short, the Nobel Prize winners have raised significant questions about the prevailing laissez-faire consensus.

Of the three economists, as the *Los Angeles Times* noted (October 11), "Stiglitz has gone the furthest in pushing the issue in policy circles and producing controversy in the process." More significantly, Stiglitz's post-1970s work, which went unremarked in his Nobel award, has gone very far in laying the foundation for a new dimension of economics incorporating asymmetries not just of information but of wealth and power.

Hours after getting the Nobel news on October 10, Stiglitz spoke to reporters about his expansive approach to economics. "I believe very strongly that economics can make a very large difference . . . for the better in the world," he said. His recent focus, he pointed out, has been on "the disparity between the haves and the have-nots," particularly on the plight of the world's poorest people. He made clear his intention to pursue those concerns vigorously. "Much of our global economic system is characterized by a lot of inequities," he said. "The global trading regime is one which has been devised mostly by the [industrialized] North for the benefit of the North. It seems to me that one of the very important elements in the agenda going forward has to be to try to redress those inequities."

Perhaps Stiglitz's most comprehensive exposition of his approach is an address he gave on "Democratic Development as the Fruits of Labor" during the January 2000 meeting of the American Economic Association in Boston. Just ending a three-year stint as chief economist at the World Bank, where he frequently challenged policies of the bank and its sister institution, the International Monetary Fund, Stiglitz reflected on how he often felt like a lone voice arguing for positions differing from those springing from neoclassical economics, particularly on policies affecting workers.

"If one didn't know better," he said in his swan song, "it might seem as if the fundamental propositions of neoclassical economics were designed to undermine the rights and positions of workers." He then went on to illustrate how several economic propositions do just that. Heading his list was this one: that labor is just another factor of production, like land and machinery, under the assumption that "there is nothing special about labor." Stiglitz offered a rebuttal in economic terms: "Labor is not like other factors. Workers have to be motivated to perform. While under some circumstances it may be difficult to coach a machine to behave in the way desired (e.g., trying to get a computer not to crash), what is entailed in eliciting the desired behavior out of a person and out of a machine are, I would argue, fundamentally different."

By using such flawed neoclassical propositions, however, policymakers sent developing countries "a standard message to increase 'labor market flexibility'," Stiglitz said. "The not so subtle subtext . . . was to lower wages and lay off unneeded workers." As a result, "even when labor market problems are not the core of the problem facing a country, all too often workers are asked to bear the brunt of the costs of adjustment."

Stiglitz, born fifty-eight years ago in Gary, Indiana, got his PhD from MIT, became a tenured professor at Yale at the age of twenty-seven, and went on to professorships at Princeton, Oxford, Stanford, and now Columbia. His experience outside academia, first as a member of President Clinton's Council of Economic Advisers and then at the World Bank, sharpened his insights into the asymmetries of wealth and power, particularly as implemented internationally under what the pros call the Washington Consensus.

The Washington Consensus is a free trade and free investment strategy for international growth first defined and labeled by Economist John Williamson in 1990. It contained no equity issues because as Williamson explained later, he found Washington policymakers "essentially contemptuous of equity concerns." Stiglitz was not among the contemptuous and is not. He argues that the Washington consensus is too narrow, economically and also morally, skewed in favor of the rich. His harshest criticism targets policies imposing and protecting the unrestricted cross-border flow of capital and then when the fleeing "hot money" creates a broader financial crisis, providing generous financial bailouts to lenders.

"In East Asia [especially during the early 1990s]," he says, "it was reckless lending by international banks and other financial institutions combined with reckless borrowing by domestic financial institutions—combined with fickle investors—that may have precipitated the crisis. But the costs, in terms of soaring unemployment and plummeting wages, were borne by workers. Workers were asked to listen to sermons about austerity and 'bearing pain' just a short while after hearing, from the same preachers, sermons about how globalization and opening up capital markets would bring them unprecedented growth."

More and more analysts see eye to eye with Stiglitz on the perils of unrestricted international capital markets. The most vocal economist among them, Jagdish Bhagwati, also a professor of economics at Columbia, identifies Wall Street by name as a guilty party and beneficiary. Even the *Economist,* in its September 28 [2001] survey of globalization, concedes that one of the clearest lessons of the past few years, is that "foreign capital is a mixed blessing," especially in the case of short-term lending and borrowing by banks, which "are systematically protected from the consequences of their reckless behavior." But unlike the *Economist,* Stiglitz presses the question of responsibility for such policies.

"Finance ministers and central bank governors have the seats at the table [of intergovernmental financial institutions]," he said in an interview published in the June 2000 *Progressive* magazine. "Finance ministers and central bank governors are linked to financial communities in their countries, so they push policies that reflect the viewpoints and interests of the financial community and barely hear the voices of those who are the first victims of dictated policies."

Stiglitz singles out the U.S. Treasury Department for blame since it shapes the U.S. position on international economic policy, which then often becomes the policy of the IMF and other intergovernmental financial institutions. At a conference convened by the AFL-CIO and the Washington College of Law last February, he said, "We would never be content to delegate domestic economic policy to the Treasury. In today's world, it is equally misguided to delegate international economic policy to the Treasury, or even to the Treasury and State. A broader range of voices, including those of labor, must be heard." That has yet to occur.

More than most economists, Stiglitz grasps that giving nongovernmental groups a voice in global economic decisions can help identify problems and find workable solutions. Organized business is often accepted in this role; organized labor is not. At a high-level meeting held in October 1991 in Shanghai, for example, the Asia-Pacific Economic Cooperation forum, an international organization of government and private leaders from the United States and twenty other Pacific Rim countries, allowed participation by business but not labor. Stiglitz believes that although business belongs at such meetings, it should not monopolize the private sector role.

Unlike some critics on the left and right who favor closing down the IMF and similar institutions, Stiglitz sticks to advocating reform. Indeed, top officials of the U.S. Treasury also seemed to be in a serious reform mode three years ago when a financial crisis was sweeping much of the world. Robert E. Rubin, then Treasury secretary, even suggested that strengthening the "architecture" of the international financial system should include implementing core labor standards throughout the world. But when the financial crisis faded, so did almost all interest by policymakers in reform.

Stiglitz holds that there is no single "best" strategy for development, that different policies impose different costs and confer different benefits on different groups, and that the choices of alternatives should be made through a democratic process. As a replacement for the Washington Consensus, he offers what he calls a new Democratic Consensus built around "democratic, equitable, and sustainable development." Among its components, he said in his Boston address, are these three principles: (1) the rights of workers should be "a central focus" of development policy, (2) "labor unions and other genuine forms of popular self-organization are key to democratic economic development," and (3) worker representatives should be heard at every level, from the workplace all the way up to the international level.

Are those ideas radical ones for a mainline economist? Not really, according to Daniel Rodrik, professor of international political economy at the Kennedy School of Government at Harvard. "What is striking about Joe's views," Rodrik wrote me in an e-mail, "is not that much their substance (similar and often more 'radical' views are expressed, using appropriate economics jargon, in academic seminars and conferences) but that they were offered by such a prominent neoclassical economist in a quasi-public forum. Economists tend to close rank, and defend the orthodoxy in their public comments, even when their own research runs counter to them."

Assails Pact He Once Advocated

(From the February 2, 2004, issue of Human Rights for Workers))

JOSEPH E. STIGLITZ, who ten years ago, as a member of the president's Council of Economic Advisers, strongly promoted the North American Free Trade Agreement (NAFTA), now says it hasn't worked out as promised. As a result, he is opposed to the Bush administration's plan to extend it to the rest of North and South America through the proposed Free Trade Area of the Americas (FTAA). He insists that the FTAA would be "an unfair trade treaty."

The 1993 trade agreement covering Canada, Mexico, and the United States was passed without "a full and open debate of [its] consequences," Stiglitz writes in "The Broken Promise of NAFTA," published in the January 6 issue of the *New York Times*. His article is obviously designed to provoke discussion at this time when "the United States [government] is bullying the weaker countries of Central and South America into accepting its terms."

As Stiglitz now sees it, NAFTA is one-sided in the generous benefits it bestows on business and capital, particularly a "new set of rights" achieved by the treaty route instead of the normal legislative process, and enforced with sanctions by secret tribunals instead of open door procedures." He explains,

> Under NAFTA, if foreign investors believe they are being harmed by regulations (no matter how well justified), they may sue for damages in special tribunals without the transparency afforded by normal judicial proceedings. If successful, they receive direct compensation from the federal government. Environmental, health, and safety regulations have been attacked and put into jeopardy. Conservatives have long sought to receive compensation for regulations that hurt them, and American courts and Congress have usually rejected these attempts. Now businesses may have accomplished indirectly, through treaty, what they could not get more openly through the democratic political process.

Meanwhile, those harmed by the actions of foreign firms, for instance by what they do to the environment, do not have comparable protections of appealing to an international tribunal and receiving compensation.

Turning to other issues in the current negotiations for FTAA and for a range of other trade agreements as well, Stiglitz faults the U.S. government for refusing to discuss agriculture and nontariff barriers while at the same time pressing "Latin American countries to compromise their national sovereignties and to agree to investor 'protections'." He attacks the U.S. demand that "countries fully liberalize their capital markets even as the International Monetary Fund has finally found that such liberalization promotes neither growth nor stabilization in developing countries."

Stiglitz's analysis of NAFTA and FTAA clashes with the conventional "free trade" beliefs espoused by most U.S. economists, embraced by Democratic and Republican administrations, and now being promulgated globally by U.S. government trade officials. Yet Stiglitz is not completely alone. Dan Rodrik of Harvard and a few lesser known economists have taken a hard look at the modern reality of globalization, and are questioning whether the theory of free trade, formulated two centuries ago, is valid in a radically changed world.

How to Judge Trade Agreements

(From the May 10, 2006, issue of Human Rights for Workers)

A NEW GUIDE for reporters covering international trade urges them to pursue questions like the following in assessing the labor content of trade agreements:

— "Do they address worker rights at all?"
— "Which worker rights are covered?"

— "Which labor rights provisions are enforceable and which are merely hortatory?"
— "Do they only require countries to enforce their existing labor laws, or do they also require that national laws meet international standards?"
— "How are labor rights requirements enforced, and what are the consequences for violating them? Fines? Trade sanctions?"
— "Are the enforcement mechanism and consequences as strong for violating labor rights provisions as for violating commercial requirements?"

So pointed and pertinent are the guide's questions that you could easily assume its publisher to be an international labor union or a worker rights advocacy group. That assumption would be wrong. The guide is published by the Initiative for Policy Dialogue, a think tank founded in 2000 by Joseph E. Stiglitz, a Nobel laureate economist. The Initiative, a global network of more than two hundred leading economists, political scientists, and others, explores policy alternatives in international development.

Titled "Covering Labor: A Reporter's Guide to Worker Rights in a Global Economy," edited Anya Schiffrin and Liza Featherstone, the guide has 113 pages of information useful not only to reporters but to policymakers who need to broaden their horizons. One of the seven chapters, "Unrepresented Workers Worldwide," is by Earl V. Brown Jr., a human rights and labor lawyer with the AFL-CIO Solidarity Center.

The new guide is part of a series published by the Initiative to give journalists the background information they need to cover complicated stories involving the world economy. Previous titles include "Covering Oil: a Reporter's Guide to Energy and Development" (with an introduction by Stiglitz), "Covering Globalization: A Handbook for Reporters," and "Business and Economic Reporting: Covering Companies, Financial Markets and the Broader Economy."

CHAPTER 15

The Delight of Sunday

After leaving full-time employment some years ago, I still found myself busy, very busy, seven days a week. One day, as I was cleaning out some old files, I ran across the photocopy of a pamphlet, "Don't Shop on Sunday," which I had written many years earlier. It started me thinking about my priorities. My reflections resulted in this article, published in the "Faith in Focus" section of *America*'s January 6-13, 2003, issue.

"STOP! DON'T SHOP on Sunday." That was the advice of a large poster hanging on a wall of our Catholic Council on Working Life office in Chicago during the 1950s. We drummed home the same message in our monthly publication, called *Work*, and in a pamphlet I wrote for Ave Maria Press. It was a modest campaign, joining the initiatives of some other groups, such as the Third Order of St. Francis, which supplied the poster. Our underlying motive was to foster respect for the Lord's Day.

Once, on a casual visit to our office, Nicholas von Hoffman, the writer who was then a community organizer on Chicago's South Side, saw the poster and shook his head skeptically. Our campaign against Sunday shopping, he predicted, would go nowhere. And he was right. It proved to be a loser.

At that time, a half century ago, only about 16 percent of supermarkets across the nation had their doors open for business on Sunday. Today, with rare exceptions, all of them do. Sunday has become their second busiest shopping day of the week, topped only by Friday or Saturday. That's the national average. In some urban neighborhoods, Sunday takes first place, not only for supermarkets, but also for department stores, auto lots, shopping malls, and other retail establishments.

From their very beginnings in the nineteenth century, U.S. unions joined with religious and other allies to maintain Sunday as very special, a day set apart from the others. Collective bargaining agreements complemented local legislation as bulwarks against the seven-day workweek. But in the mid-1900s retail businesses and consumers increased pressures to make Sunday another day of commerce. In opposing that trend, Patrick E. Gorman, then head of a Chicago-based national union of food workers, wrote, "There is absolutely no excuse for Sunday operation in any food market. The whole idea is irreligious . . . . With all of the modern conveniences for home storage of meats and other perishables, there is no plausible reason [for food store openings on Sunday]."

At that time, some businesses' leaders in the retail industry felt the same way. A grocery chain executive, G. L. Clements of the Jewel Tea Company, said that his company "has a firm belief that it can give service to homemakers in six days of business, and [that] no additional benefits are to be derived from remaining open on Sunday." Some businesses joined with unions and churches to support Sunday closing laws. Arguing that "Sunday is a holy day, a family day," a grocery store owners' association in Pueblo, Colorado, for example, backed a proposed ordinance to ban Sunday food sales, but voters defeated it by a two to one margin.

In support of its theme, "Don't Shop on Sundays," my pamphlet quoted Gorman, Clements, church leaders, and others who, futilely, as it turned out, opposed the growing trend. In fact, I went back to an 1884 pastoral letter issued by the plenary council in Baltimore to quote a warning of the U.S. bishops: "To turn the

Lord's day into a day of toil is a blighting curse to a country." But the foundation of my case rested on this long quotation excerpted from the Bible (Exodus 20:8-11): "Remember that thou keep holy the Sabbath day. Six days shalt thou labor and shalt do all thy works. But the seventh day is the Sabbath of the Lord thy God. Thou shalt do no work on it, nor thy son nor thy daughter, nor thy manservant nor thy maidservant, nor thy beast nor the stranger that is within thy gates. For in six days the Lord made heaven and earth and the sea and all things that are in them, and rested on the seventh day."

Notice that as laid down in Exodus, God's law on a weekly day of nonwork has both an individual and a social dimension. Together, they mean that I am morally responsible not just for my own conduct on Sunday and how it affects *me*, but also for how it affects *others*—arguably including those drawn into Sunday work by my shopping in a supermarket or auto salesroom. The *Catechism of the Catholic Church* does not quote Exodus's strong prohibition against having others work for me on Sunday, but it does say, "Every Christian should avoid making unnecessary demands on others that would hinder them from observing the Lord's Day."

Here I should admit that my pamphlet's excerpt from Exodus was not as complete as it could have been. I neglected to include both what the Lord tells Moses to tell the Israelites, "Anyone who does work on the Sabbath day shall be put to death" (Exodus 31:14), and how Moses relayed that instruction word for word (Exodus 35:2). Why had I left out this powerful warning that violations of the Sabbath merited death? Frankly, at the time I had not read far enough into Exodus. Even if I had done so, however, I probably would not have quoted this passage. Why not? Because doing so would have prompted puzzlement and disbelief among those I was trying to persuade. (*Capital punishment for Sunday shopping? Gimme a break.*) One rule about writing that I learned early on was to avoid introducing issues that you can't deal with convincingly in the space available.

In any case, how persuasive are arguments based solely on fear of a dire punishment? Were I to update my Ave Maria pamphlet, which has long been out of print, it would have a more positive theme. Unfortunately, when I wrote it a half century ago, I was not familiar with the profound wisdom of Isaiah and the positive emphasis that he put on the "delight" of observing Sunday as a holy day. I would certainly have quoted that great prophet's words (58:13-14):

> If you hold back your foot on the Sabbath from following
> your own pursuits on my holy day:
> If you call the Sabbath a delight and the Lord's holy day
> honorable;
> If you honor it by not following your ways, seeking your
> own interests, or speaking with malice—
> Then you shall delight in the Lord, and I will make you
> ride on the heights of the earth.

Here Isaiah not only recognizes the Lord's Day as *different* but promises soaring happiness if I respect that difference by pursuing a special path, different from the paths I ordinarily follow six days of my week. Like other biblical truths, this guideline is fundamentally simple and still profoundly challenging to the consciences of different people in different circumstances.

Even though Isaiah's words offer no moral blueprint, they don't leave anyone off the hook either. Each of us should ask, "What does it mean for me in my own special circumstances at this time in my life?" I've asked myself that question again and again of late. In my seven decades on this earth, the Lord has been very good to me, so good that I've often wondered, "*Why me*, O Lord, why me?" I was able to withdraw from the job market more than a decade ago, thanks to Social Security and other pension checks generous enough so that I don't need income even from a part-time job. I now have at my disposal rest and leisure seven days a week.

In these comfortable circumstances, however, I've continued to work, not to make money, but to make some use of the knowledge and skills I've developed over the years. In a real sense, my whole life has been an apprenticeship for what I'm doing now: writing on human rights issues, occasionally for magazines, but mainly for my own Web site [and Web blog], Human Rights for Workers, which is now in its seventh year. Altogether, it is one senior citizen's personal contribution to the cause that John Paul II calls "globalizing human solidarity."

The First Psalm says, "Happy indeed is the man . . . whose delight is the law of the Lord and who ponders his law day and night." Personally, I am happy indeed that I have been blessed with the weeklong freedom to ponder the meaning of God's law for many of today's global issues and to write about some of them. But, respecting Isaiah's wisdom, I still strive to revere Sunday as very special. Without the need to round up children for Sunday mass together, I can easily arrive fifteen or twenty minutes early to review the readings of the day and to meditate on them. On Sundays I refrain from paying bills, balancing the checkbook, shopping at stores or online, working in the garden, washing the car, and doing similar nonemergency chores. Now I have plenty of time to do such those things during the six other days of the week. When I was employed, I did not have that choice. At least I thought I didn't.

I remember that as youngsters at home, my sisters and I were not allowed to read the comics before mass. The comics no longer interest me, before or after mass, but the news and features in the Sunday papers do. I clip articles having special relevance to my daily work, but I don't write articles or business letters. Sunday is a good time for writing personal letters to family members and friends. Time too for visiting our grandsons and granddaughter nearby and to phone those more distant. Time to read and reflect on a chapter of a good book on the New Testament.

The overriding goal is to make Sunday a day to tread a path truly different from, and perhaps less hectic than, those taken on the other days of the week. I cannot claim I'm always successful. But in case you're wondering, this article was researched, written, and edited on weekdays.

CHAPTER 16

Marked Failure

The scandal of defective imports from China grabbed public attention in the last half of 2007. Hastily drawn plans to protect consumers, however, neglected to take into account that the dimension of the problem is global and therefore requires a global response. Human Rights for Workers commented on this failure in several articles, starting with the first one below, which was headlined "Protecting People from Dangerous Imports" in the October 2007 issue.

SHAKEN BY CONTINUING revelations of contaminated food and other unsafe products from China, the *New York Times* issued a strong call for protecting American consumers against dangerous imports. In a two-part editorial on September 16, the *Times* went to great lengths to explain "the need for regulation for all of the nation's imports . . . and especially our children's toys."

The *Times* assessment of the need was correct. Unfortunately, its recommendations for addressing the need left a big hole. Reforms are needed all along today's vast global production and distribution chain—involving all the numerous parties responsible for its operation. The *Times* listed some of these global parties, including the original manufacturers, importers, wholesalers, retailers, the respective governments, and their inspection agencies; and it identified those that especially need to improve consumer protection.

One is the U.S. government and its newly created interagency working group on import safety. In record time, the group issued a twenty-two-page brochure on a "strategic framework" for improving import safety, but was it mostly a PR exercise?

The editorial's view: "The administration's record provides grounds for skepticism." The administration's approach—of relying almost entirely on businesses to regulate themselves—"has not worked." Instead, "American toy makers must be truly regulated by a well-financed, powerful [U.S. Consumer Product Safety Commission]."

Important as such a reform could be, it would not be up to coping with a problem that is global in dimension. Mattel, for example, has had to recall products not only in the United States but also in Europe and some Latin American countries. Parents in Italy and Chile are just as troubled as those in America. As a result, the European Union's consumer protection commissioner is considering an import ban on toys and some other products made in China. The EU is also exchanging views with the U.S. Consumer Product Safety Commission on how to "ensure that our messages to China are mutually reinforced."

But bilateral—or trilateral—measures are inadequate for addressing the global challenge. The *Times,* long an advocate of multilateralism for coping with global challenges, should realize that.

In a letter to the *Times* editor on September 16, I developed that point as follows:

> Your recommendation for improving U.S. *domestic* regulation of imports is designed for the past, not for a world economy transformed by a vast expansion in world trade. In 1960 the United States imported goods worth $14.8 million for the whole year. Last year, our imports of goods totaled $1,861.4 million—a 125-fold expansion.

During each month this year our imports of products from China alone are far exceeding our imports from the whole world in twelve months of 1960.

Yes, the present system of *domestic* regulation of imports desperately needs improvement, but that system alone doesn't suffice for the transformed world economy of the twenty-first century. Domestic regulation needs to be complemented by international regulation that, at the very minimum, protects our children against dangerous toys, contaminated food, and other unsafe products.

The international trade and investment system—through a huge network of multilateral, regional, bilateral, and plurilateral agreements—is designed to advance and protect the interests of international commerce. How long will it take to recognize that enforceable international safeguards of product safety are harmonious with the interests of commerce?

The *Times* did not publish any letter commenting on its editorial. That's too bad because the issues it raised deserve wide debate. The *Times*, like the media generally, seems allergic to fostering a serious debate about globalization.

Bad Policies, Bad Results

(From the December 2007 issue of Human Rights for Workers)

"JOIN US IN sending a message urging Congress to keep America safe this summer," said the appeal e-mailed on November 15 from the magazine, *Consumer Reports*. More than 275,000 persons had already signed a letter to Congress demanding it stop unsafe imports. I followed their lead after tweaking a sample letter.

Later, after rereading that letter, I had some second thoughts. I expressed them in this e-mail to Jim Guest, president of the Consumers Union, which publishes *Consumer Reports*.

I support your initiative to "keep hazardous products OUT of U.S." I sent your form letter to the decision makers in Congress, and I had it forwarded to close relatives and a friend in hopes that they too would put pressure on Congress to act. I did so instinctively out of concern for the children in my family and in other American families. But it now dawns on me: *what about the children—and the adults—in the rest of the world?* The contaminated consumer goods that concern you and me—the pet food, the dolls, the toys, the jewelry, and the rest—are all outputs of a vast global production and marketing system unprecedented in its scope. Take the poisonous toy beads called Aqua Dogs in North America and Bindez I in Asia.

As reported in a November 11 New York Times article ("China Confirms Poison Was on Toy Beads"), the beads are made in the southeastern city of Shenzhen in China, in a factory owned by a Taiwanese toy manufacturer with a contracting office in Hong Kong; are distributed to about forty countries across Asia and Europe by Moose Enterprises, a company in Australia; and are marketed in North America by a company in Toronto, Canada, Spin Master. That listing leaves out the subcontractor in China that may have supplied the poisonous glue for the beads. Globalized problems cry to be addressed in a globalized way. Yes, we must protect Americans from poisonous imports, but what about people in the rest of the world?

We don't know how many children have died or been injured by this glue and other poisons in products sold this year in the United States and around the world. We may never know. But we do know, or should know, that the United States cannot handle this alone, or even in cooperation with Europe. Nor, in this highly competitive global marketplace, can manufacturers and retailers do so. The intergovernmental organization that regulates cross-border trade in goods and services, the World Trade Organization, must be involved.

Why the reluctance to recognize the WTO's responsibility? I am afraid that our decision makers are restrained by their belief in free trade ideology—a belief that in its own way is as poisonous as the glue found in Aqua Dots.

The Consumers Union is far from alone in taking an insular approach. The *New York Times* does too.

In an editorial titled "Reform and Consumer Safety," the November 19 *Times* urged Congress to pass a "law that would force reform on an agency [the Consumer Protection Safety Commission] that for too long has been led by foot-dragging political appointees." Good idea. The editorial also criticized industry lobbyists and the Bush administration for fighting effective reforms that put consumer safety first. Also a good idea although the private toy companies deserve a public shaming for their lobbyists' actions.

Missing from the editorial was any recognition that this scandal has a global dimension that affects consumers across the world. At least in this case, it should be uncontested that global integration needs global regulation.

The continuing global problem of unsafe imports illustrates the main characteristics of unfettered globalization: (1) that governments rely on twentieth century means to cope with twenty-first-century realities; and (2) that corporations, more adaptive, are therefore able to exploit rights that are not balanced by corresponding responsibilities.

—

CHAPTER 17

Correcting a Blind Spot

One of the significant social developments in the past two decades is the growing recognition that the basic worker rights—particularly the right to form a union and to have that union act as the representative of workers—are human rights. Oddly, human rights organizations were not pioneers in promoting that view. The change is described in these articles, compiled from the August 1, 2003, and February 1, 2005, issues of Human Rights for Workers.

IT APPEARED ABOUT twenty years ago, in a dark blue loose-leaf binder, a format too modest to call a "publication." As editor, I called it a handbook and titled it *Handbook for Trade Union and Other Human Rights,* with the subtitle "Source Material on Universal Rights Affecting Working Men and Women." Its forward by AFL-CIO president Lane Kirkland, excerpted from one of his speeches, explained the human and political values involved as follows:

> Freedom of association is a universal human right. To suppress it is to cripple working men and women, as well as the country in which they live, developed or developing, East or West, North or South.

> The right to organize is essential to healthy economic and
> political development. It is the foundation of all other
> human rights. For without the right to band together in
> self-defense, the people are powerless to defend their
> rights to free speech, free worship, free elections, free
> emigration, or any other right that the strong might take
> from the weak.

The handbook had eighty-five pages, mostly devoted to the texts
of sixteen conventions of the UN's International Labor Organization,
starting with five on the right to organize, plus practical suggestions
on how to work for those rights. The Asian-American Free Labor
Institute, an AFL-CIO branch for which I then worked as a program
officer, distributed the handbook in Asia as well to AFL-CIO affiliates
in the United States.

The handbook made a modest contribution to correcting an
intellectual blind spot about labor. It demonstrated that worker
rights, including the right to unionize, are human rights and
should be respected as such in public policy, both nationally and
internationally. That key idea, long promulgated by the labor
movements of the world, today is accepted by some influential
human rights organizations that back in 1986 had a narrower
perspective.

Among those groups, none has done more to correct the blind
spot than the New York City-based Human Rights Watch. During its
first fifteen years of life, worker rights issues were missing from its
agenda. Its executive director during that period, Aryeh Neier, made
a sharp distinction between "civil and political rights," on the one
hand, and "economic and social rights" on the other. In his book,
Taking Liberties, subtitled "Four Decades in the Struggle for Rights"
(first with the American Civil Liberties Union and then with Human
Rights Watch), Neier notes that he "strenuously opposed efforts" to
get Human Rights Watch involved in "economic issues as rights." For
him, "economic issues" do not merit "the language of rights."

After Neier left Human Rights Watch in 1993, its vision became
more inclusive. Under its mission, "protecting the human rights

of people around the world," it now explicitly recognizes the key conventions of the UN's International Labor Organization as part of international human rights law. In August 2000, for example, it broke new ground with a study titled *Unfair Advantage: Workers' Freedom of Association in the United States under International Human Rights Standards,* written by Lance Compa, teacher, writer, former union official, and longtime worker rights activist.

The 217-page report, as Human Rights Watch executive director Kenneth Roth said in a press release, described in heavily researched detail how "the cards are stacked against workers in the United States." Documenting that fact alone was a major achievement, but Compa did more than that. He marshaled the legal, moral, and other talents of Human Rights Watch to analyze how the state of worker rights in the United States often conflicted with the values that, thanks partly to American leadership, are enshrined in the international human rights norms of the United Nations and the International Labor Organization.

In Cornell University Press's 2004 paperback edition of *Unfair Advantage,* Compa writes, "The reality of labor law and practice in the United States . . . has not changed much since the report's initial publication in 2000." Still, despite the fact that "many workers who try to exercise the right to organize still suffer widespread harassment, threats, spying, and dismissals for their efforts," he considers it "remarkable that each year hundreds of thousands of workers overcome those obstacles to form new local unions in U.S. workplaces." He explains why:

> The organizing impulse springs from a bedrock of human need for association in a common purpose to make things better, as corny as that sounds and amid predominantly individualistic social pressures. Polls indicate that more than 40,000,000 workers would join unions immediately in their workplaces if they did not risk reprisals from employers.

What if many more people were to recognize that worker rights are human rights? Would that change U.S. law and practice? No, that alone won't bring about change, Compa says in the book's final paragraphs. "A human rights approach brings a new dimension that [and new allies who] can begin a process of change—*can*, not 'will,' and *begin*, not 'finish.' . . . Changing the climate is a necessary prelude to changing law, policy, and practice."

So if a greater understanding of human rights is insufficient, what other climactic changes are needed to make progress on worker rights? Answering that crucial question is beyond the scope of Compa's book and this particular Human Rights Watch report. One answer, in my view, is to embed worker rights in international trade policy. And on this subject, unwisely ignored by many social justice groups, Human Rights Watch is also making a values-based contribution. In the past three years, it has issued three statements exposing the unfairness of the U.S.-Central American Free Trade Agreement (CAFTA), the last being its March 2004 briefing paper titled "CAFTA's Weak Labor Rights Protections: Why the Present Accord Should Be Opposed."

Revisiting "The Jungle"

> "They love you if you're healthy and work like a dog, but if you get hurt, you are trash . . . They will look for a way to get rid of you before they report [the injury to authorities]. They will find a reason to fire you or put you on a worse job . . . or change your shift so you quit. So a lot of people don't report their injuries. They just work with the pain."

THAT WAS THE testimony of a worker at the Nebraska beef plant worker in Omaha who was interviewed for a new Human Rights Watch report, *Blood, Sweat, and Fear: Workers' Rights in U.S. Meat and Poultry Plants.* With an injury rate more than three times that of U.S. private industry as a whole, "Meatpacking is the most dangerous factory job in America," says Lance Compa, author of the report and a labor researcher for Human Rights Watch. "Dangerous conditions are cheaper for companies—and the government does next to nothing." Field research for the report concentrated on beef packing in Nebraska, hog slaughtering in North Carolina, and poultry processing in Arkansas, with a close look at Tyson Foods Inc., Smithfield Foods Inc., and Nebraska Beef Ltd.

Besides inflicting dangerous working conditions, the industry generally hampers its workers by its aggressive hostility to unions. Workers who "try to form trade unions and bargain collectively are spied on, harassed, pressured, threatened, suspended, fired, deported, or otherwise victimized for their exercise of the right to freedom of association," the report states. "Labor laws that are supposed to protect worker rights have fundamental gaps, and government agencies fail to enforce effectively those laws that do purport to protect workers' rights."

Immigrant workers, who form a large part of the industry's workforce, are especially vulnerable, the report emphasizes. First of all, most are unaware of their rights, and then because many are here illegally or have undocumented family members, they are afraid to make their grievances known to government authorities. "Employers take advantage of these fears to keep workers in abusive conditions that violate basic human rights and labor rights," the report states.

"Every country has its horrors," Jamie Fellner, director of the U.S. program at Human Rights Watch, told the *New York Times,* "and this industry is one of the horrors in the United States."

Upton Sinclair's classic novel *The Jungle* exposed the horrors of meatpacking plants a century ago, and the shocked public reaction led directly to the rapid passage of the Pure Food and Drug Act and the Federal Meat Inspection Act of 1906.

Blood, Sweat, and Fear has a whole chapter containing detailed recommendations on how employers, the Congress, the executive branch, and state governments can end the industry's current horrors. Among its eleven recommendations to Congress, for example, are these two, neither of which has yet passed (as of late 2008):

> Enact the Wrongful Death Accountability Act to strengthen criminal penalties for willful violations of the Occupational Safety and Health Act that cause worker fatalities. Currently, willful violations resulting in death are nothing more than misdemeanors with a maximum sentence of six months.

> Enact the Employee Free Choice Act (EFCA) amending the National Labor Relations Act to provide stronger protection for workers' freedom of association and stronger remedies for violations. The EFCA provides for the determination of workers' choice of bargaining representatives by an orderly, nonadversarial process of signing cards to authorize union bargaining instead of the fear-filled and delay-ridden NLRB election process; a neutral arbitration system for first-contract bargaining impasses in newly organized workplaces; stronger penalties for violations of the Act; and more vigorous use of injunctive remedies to have unfairly dismissed workers reinstated to their jobs quickly, instead of waiting years while employers appeal their cases.

This is the season when many religious publications recommend spiritual books to be read during Lent. *Blood, Sweat, and Fear* belongs on that list, at least for people striving for a spirituality that has genuine biblical roots, particularly in the Lord's foretelling of Judgment Day (Matthew 26:31-40).

CHAPTER 18

Corporate Social Responsibility

In the past decade, concern about business involvement in labor issues has grown so much, even among corporate managers, that corporate social responsibility has gained its own acronym and recognition as a movement as well. The first article in this chapter, drawing partly from material on my Human Rights for Workers Web site, was published in the winter 2007 issue of *Dissent* under the above title. I probed the subject further in the second article here, posted on February 12, 2008, on my new blog, also named Human Rights for Workers.

IN HIS BEST-SELLING book *Capitalism and Freedom,* first published in 1962, future Nobel laureate and world-renowned economist Milton Friedman laid down this basic principle for corporate executives: their sole social responsibility is to maximize the income and wealth of stockholders. "Few trends," he wrote, "could so thoroughly undermine the very foundations of our free society as the acceptance by corporate officials of a social responsibility other than to make as much money for their stockholders as possible. This is a fundamentally subversive doctrine."

Union leaders, student activists, environmentalists, and advocates of various other types have long accepted that subversive doctrine. Of late, more and more top corporate officials, despite their own large stockholdings, have also done so. Though only a tiny minority, they stand out publicly as pioneers in venturing outside the business path dedicated solely to maximizing the financial well-being of shareholders. Even in the business world, "the movement for corporate social responsibility has won the battle of ideas," according to the *Economist*, the English-language media's foremost defender of capitalism.

In a January 22, 2005, editorial and eighteen-page article, both titled "The Good Company," the *Economist* formally joined the battle on Friedman's side (without invoking his name) and exhorted corporation leaders to reject the notion of corporate social responsibility (CSR). Quoting the idealized self-interest of Adam Smith's butcher, brewer, and baker, the lengthy article dismissed CSR as "based on a faulty—and dangerously faulty—analysis of the capitalist system," and hence a tool for wrongful interference in corporate decision making. The company that works within the law, and doesn't cheat, "is doing good works" just by making a profit, the *Economist* insisted. A corporation can be a "good company" without the cosmetics of CSR.

Like any fledgling movement, CSR has many different manifestations. In one way or other, however, the common thread running through CSR is the idea of somehow integrating the public interest into the corporation's mission. The *Economist* fired both barrels at this core idea. "There is much to be said for leaving social and economic policy to governments. They, at least, are accountable to voters," it editorialized (inconveniently ignoring the governments of China and Vietnam). And it wound up its eighteen-pager with this wisdom: "The proper guardians of the public interest are governments . . . . The proper business of business is business. No apology required."

And yet the movement keeps moving, both inside and outside the business world. Most troubling of all, from the Friedman/*Economist* perspective, is how widely CSR has infiltrated the executive suite itself. For example, as the magazine pointed out, in their annual reports most large multinational now justify their existence in terms of "service to the community," rather than merely in profit terms. It is one thing for Amnesty International and the Evangelical Lutheran Church to embrace CSR. It is another for a multinational corporation like Sprint Nextel to appoint a vice president in charge of corporate social responsibilities.

Some business leaders have gone so far as to become active in nongovernmental organizations that promote CSR principles and practice. Business for Social Responsibility, founded by San Francisco corporate executives, attracted more than seven hundred business people to Chicago for its conference in November 2005 (when a *New York Times* ten-page advertising supplement on social responsibility featured full-page ads of AstraZeneca, ExxonMobil, Pfizer, and Starbucks).

Perhaps even more significant is the growing acceptance of CSR principles by intergovernmental organizations. The UN Global Compact, a "corporate citizenship" project first proposed by UN General Secretary Kofi Annan in 1999, has gained the participation of more than 2,300 business firms in eighty-seven countries. Another UN-born proposal, a set of proposed global norms on human rights for multinational corporations and their related business enterprises, is being debated in the new Human Rights Council. In his interim report as the UN secretary-general's special representative for business and human rights, Professor John G. Ruggie of Harvard wrote, "At the level of the world political economy as a whole, policymakers and pundits of varying persuasions are coming to appreciate a lesson that history taught us long ago: severe imbalances between the scope of markets and business organizations on the one hand, and the capacity of societies to protect and promote core values of social community on the other, are not sustainable."

A recent CSR breakthrough on the intergovernmental level came in two steps last year [2006]. On the first of May, the International Finance Corporation (IFC), the World Bank's private lending arm, put into effect comprehensive labor and environmental standards covering the $5,000,000,000 it invests annually in the private sector across the globe. The plan "is to influence markets, not just [its own] projects and clients," the IFC said. Toward that end, it announced in August that it is teaming up with the UN International Labor Organization to promote better labor standards in the global garment, footwear, electronic equipment, and other light manufacturing industries.

Another sign of the way the wind seems to be blowing is a new development at the International Standards Organization (ISO), a quasi-official network of the standards institutes of 157 countries, which has formalized over sixteen thousand global standards, each with its own ISO number. The ISO is now developing an international standard with guidelines on "social responsibility," including the right to unionize. It has already has its own ID—ISO 26000, with 2008 as its publication date. "The need for organizations in both public and private sectors to behave in a socially responsible way," the ISO explains, "is becoming a generalized requirement of society."

In a far-reaching kind of CSR initiative, representatives from the business, academic, legal, labor, government, and investor communities are working together in a long-term project called Corporation 2020. Launched in Boston two years ago, it is addressing this question: in a just society, how should the future corporation be constituted to ensure that it serves the long-term common good, rather than short-term shareholder interests? As Allen L. White, cofounder of Corporation 2020, puts it, "The sheer weight of the corporate role in wealth creation and the footprint associated with this creative process makes responsibility inevitable . . . . The core question facing companies is how to harness the full potential of business to serve the public interest while preserving and enhancing core assets—creativity, innovation, and competitive drive."

Note that all this diverse CSR activity focuses almost entirely on the level of *ideas*. But what effect does it have out in the real world? Does it make any difference in the daily operations of the world's 78,000 multinational firms, their roughly 780,000 foreign affiliates, and their millions of suppliers and distributors in China and elsewhere?

The key testing ground for the CSR movement is the global network of production and supply chains that serve multinational corporations with products from factories they do not own, made by many millions of workers they do not employ, in countries whose culture they do not share. Ideas can have consequences, at least eventually, but so far there is no evidence that CSR ideas have mattered much in this network, which is the breeding ground of sweatshops. Yes, there are a few strands of progress—for example, Nike is now disclosing the names and locations of overseas factories making its sneakers—but no advocate can claim that more than a decade of CSR has delivered on the promise inherent in its ideas.

- At a recent (June 2006) Bangkok meeting on monitoring and correcting abuses in the global supply chain, Govindasamy Rajasekaran, secretary-general of the Malaysian Trades Union Congress, reported that only a very small minority of companies in Asia have implemented CSR policies for the millions of workers employed by their contractors and subcontractors.
- Using the multinational's own voluminous data on internal audits of eight hundred Nike suppliers in fifty-one countries, a Sloan Management School research team conducted a study titled "Does Monitoring Improve Labor Standards? Lessons from Nike." The short answer: no. Though praising Nike for its effort to improve working conditions among its suppliers, the study concluded that monitoring "is not producing the significant and sustained improvement in workplace conditions that many had hoped."
- Based on extensive experience in monitoring factories in Latin America and Asia, Garrett Brown, an occupational health and safety professional, wrote in the September 2005 issue of *Industrial Safety and Hygiene News*. "The experience over the last decade with 'operationalizing' corporate social responsibility beyond glossy annual reports indicates very little tangible progress has been made."

So there may be a good deal of truth in the cynical judgment that the *Economist* expressed in its "The Good Company" article: "For most

---

companies . . . CSR is little more than a cosmetic treatment. The human face that CSR applies to capitalism goes on each morning, gets increasingly smeared by day, and washes off at night."

Alternatively, the *Economist* may have been on to something in another judgment it reached in the same article: that "the proper guardians of the public interest are governments." Could it be that, to attain its goals in the global economy, CSR needs help from governments?

A CSR-diligent company can certainly use external help in applying its principles. That is illustrated by the experience of a Reebok human rights monitor recounted in "Our Commitment to Human Rights," Reebok's 2005 CSR report (the last one it made before Germany's giant athletic goods marketer, Adidas, bought it). Sherry Yan, a human rights monitor directly responsible for inspecting forty of the 160 or more factories in Reebok's China supply chain, wrote, "I love my job, but it can be very frustrating, especially when there is nothing I can do [to make changes that last]. For example, even when I have helped reduce [excessive] working hours in a factory once, the problem occurs again because of the pressure of the industry . . . . I hope other brands come on board so that I am not always seen as the bad guy with factory management. If more brands collaborated on this, we could really make a difference in the lives of workers."

Some companies do manage to collaborate with each other to advance CSR goals. For example, eleven multinationals have joined a "Business Leaders Initiative on Human Rights," and are doing test runs in applying the draft UN multinational human rights norms to their own firms. But profit-maximizing competition on the international level is intrinsically incompatible with pro-CSR solidarity. After all, a multinational that is devoted to CSR is at a disadvantage in competing with multinationals that are not, given a global marketplace with rules that grant them awesome rights without any corresponding responsibilities or accountability.

Occasionally a worried corporate executive, with nowhere else to turn, calls on government for help. A senior official of Google did so in February [2006] when he was on the hot seat at a congressional hearing investigating why U.S.-based Internet companies are actively cooperating with China's strict censorship policies. Elliott Schrage, a Google vice president, testified that the U.S. Department of State and Commerce and the Office of the U.S. Trade Representative "should treat censorship as a barrier to trade." He advocated making "[anti-] censorship a central element of our bilateral and multilateral [trade] agendas."

Brad Adams, Asia director of Human Rights Watch, commented, "Laws are needed to end this race to the bottom and establish a level playing field so that the Chinese government can't pick off companies one by one. Otherwise, the standard set will be that of the company trying the hardest to please the Chinese government." But the new U.S. laws recommended in Human Rights Watch's report on the problem, "Race to the Bottom: Corporate Complicity in Chinese Internet Censorship," did not include any change in trade policies.

Governments have long resisted adding a human rights (or CSR-like) dimension to the global trading regime, as embodied in the world, regional, subregional, and bilateral trade agreements that span the globe. In their 2003 book, *Can Labor Standards Improve Under Globalization?*, Kimberly Ann Elliott of the Institute for International Economics and Richard B. Freeman of Harvard recommended that the World Trade Organization outlaw trade-related violations of core labor standards, just as it has outlawed trade-related violations of intellectual property rights. They specifically urged that the WTO zero in on the world's export processing zones (now estimated to employ 67,000,000 workers, most of them women) and transform the zones into "globalization at its best." The WTO remained unmoved, partly because of the objections of governments in third world countries, even though the unions in some of them support the proposal.

In one area of international law, third world governments have a clear and direct stake in reform. That is the global network of treaties and agreements protecting foreign investment and investors. As they now stand, these special (and little publicized) types of international agreements grant a wide range of rights and privileges to foreign investors without any corresponding responsibilities or accountability while also imposing a wide range of obligations on host governments without corresponding rights. The one-sided licenses thus granted to mining and energy multinationals, for example, go far to explain the "resource curse" that is so puzzling to some economists.

The Canada-based International Institute for Sustainable Development has developed a comprehensive case for changing that imbalance while still promoting investment. After intensively studying foreign investment issues facing developing countries, the Institute prepared a draft "Model International Agreement for Sustainable Development." As its preamble states, the model agreement seeks to create "an overall balance of rights and obligations in international investment between investors, host countries, and home countries." In its mix of binding and voluntary responsibilities, the model urges the host state to have laws and policies consistent with the ILO's 1998 declaration on core worker rights and requires investors to follow those laws and policies. Howard Mann, a coauthor of the model, explains, "One can argue about many of the details, but we believe that the fundamental principle is unassailable: it is never a good thing to have rights without obligations."

It is never a good thing to have rights without obligations. That yardstick should be utilized in reassessing the whole range of present and future trade agreements, from the "multilateral" ones of the World Trade Organization to the regional and the many bilateral ones of the United States and other countries. Objectively carried out, that reassessment could generate reforms filling a major gap that was built into the global trading regime from its very start at the end of World War II.

By that time, it had become obvious to top leaders of the United States and other Western nations that the laws and agencies of individual countries were grossly inadequate for the postwar growth in cross-border commerce. In 1947, by adopting the General Agreement on Tariffs and Trade (GATT), the WTO's forerunner, they filled an institutional and legal gap in the international marketplace—but they did so very partially, in two senses of the word:

partial as in incomplete and *partial* as in favoring one group over others. GATT addressed the rights and interests of one important group—the multinational business firms, banks, law offices, and allied firms headquartered in the United States, Western Europe, and Japan—but ignored a group essential to global production: the men, women, and children in the international labor market.

GATT's incompleteness, its partiality, established a worker-*un*friendly template for the whole system of multilateral, regional, subregional, bilateral, and plurilateral (don't ask) trade and investment agreements that followed.

Ideally, the International Labor Organization, founded just after World War I, could have been modernized after World War II, but leading government and employer representatives—both active under the ILO's unique "tripartite" structure—kept the ILO frozen in its 1918 mode, radically unfit to promote and defend worker interests in the global economy. True, employer and government representatives, worried by increasing pressures to get the sanctions-equipped WTO involved in also protecting the rights of workers, joined forces to gain unanimous approval in 1998 for the "ILO Declaration on Fundamental Principles and Rights at Work and Its Follow-Up." It is an impressive document on core worker rights, except that the prescribed follow-up, already weak in substance, has been even weaker in implementation. The United States government, unequaled in potential influence to translate those rights into practice, has chosen not to do so, under both Democratic and Republican administrations. The same benighted bipartisanship has kept the United States from adopting the ILO conventions on freedom of association and the right of collective bargaining.

So it is no wonder that multinational corporations prosper under rules and regulations that bestow on them global rights, privileges, and powers without any corresponding global responsibilities or accountability. Yes, most trade agreements now do give verbal recognition to labor rights, but in meaningless ways, without the protections that international agreements and agencies routinely guarantee to capital. It should not come as an utter surprise, therefore, that businesses, in a "rational" pursuit of their interests, take full advantage of a global economy that leaves them free of any "social responsibility other than to make as much money for their stockholders as possible."

The system is working as designed. In two issues last year (2006), *Forbes* listed a record number of people worth at least one billion dollars—793 in the whole world, and in the United States alone, all four hundred among the four hundred richest Americans. Naturally, workers are getting a smaller slice of the economic pie: the portion of the U.S. economy going to workers in wages and benefits declined by 2.5 percentage points, reaching a low of 56.5 percent of the gross domestic product while the decline was even greater in Germany (3.1 percentage points) and Japan (3 percentage points) during roughly the same period.

"The usual argument in favor of globalization—that it will make most workers better off, with only a few low-skilled ones losing out—has not so far been borne out by the facts," the *Economist* wrote in its September 16, 2006, survey of the world economy. Uncharacteristically, the seventeen-page survey suggested that "the traditional trade model needs modification," but it suppressed that notion in listing its recommendations for countering the political backlash against globalization. It stuck to remedies confined to the domestic scene, such as better education for tomorrow's jobs and "more flexible labor markets." But the need to reform international trade *internationally* cannot be sloughed off that easily.

The United States, as a government and as a people, will have to confront that need directly because of the expiration in mid-2007 of the controversial 304-page "trade promotion authority" legislation that Congress enacted by a paper-thin 215-212 margin at three o'clock one morning in July 2002. For the duration of its five-year term, that legislation accelerates the passage of the president's trade bills—and related domestic legislation—through Congress without amendment, without the usual congressional hearings, and with very limited floor debate in the House and Senate (hence the popular name "fast track"). Thereby, the Bush administration has had a lot of leeway to put its own corporate-friendly imprint on the country's own trade policy *and* on the policy that the U.S.

government zealously promotes throughout the global trade and investment system.

The upcoming debate on whether to change that policy will show where the corporate social responsibility movement really stands. Will it expose CSR as just a cosmetic?

Five years ago, amid a prolonged period of antiglobalization demonstrations, Boeing, Caterpillar, and other big U.S. exporters began reconsidering what *Business Week* called "their implacable opposition" to linking labor rights and world trade rules. Even the muscular corporate lobby, the Business Roundtable, seemed interested, but the Bush administration and House GOP leaders were not.

To date, only *one* U.S. corporation—Levi Strauss & Co.—has come out unequivocally in support of such a linkage. Here are the key paragraphs of Levi Strauss's policy statement on "progressive trade liberalization":

> We firmly believe that labor provisions—including key workplace standards and worker rights provisions, with effective enforcement measures—should be an integral part of all bilateral, regional, or multilateral trade negotiations to protect worker rights in an environment of increasing globalization. We are a leader in publicly and effectively advocating this position and have been doing so since 2000.

> We are resolute in our commitment that future trade agreements must include strong language on labor protection at their core. These protections should include effective measures and processes to ensure compliance—including recourse under the World Trade Organization dispute settlement proceedings if necessary—to enforce them.

Back in 1998, when it was taking constant heat for its sweatshops, Nike said that it needed government help to get supplier factories to follow its code of conduct on freedom of association and the right to collective bargaining. Its Web posting (which has since disappeared) explained that "advocacy by governments who believe that these rights should be upheld globally is a tremendously powerful tool [to] press intransigent peers to recognize these rights through international forums and other forms of diplomatic pressure." But the statement stopped short of recognizing that trade rules are a powerful tool.

Today Nike has nearly 150 employees engaged in full-time or significant part-time CSR activities under the slogan of "Do the Right Thing." Isn't it about time for Nike, if it takes CSR seriously, to do the right thing by publicly endorsing the need for a worker rights dimension in trade agreements? If more companies did so, it would transform the upcoming debate on U.S. trade policy.

Resetting the direction of that policy to make it worker friendly is a crucial national challenge. Another challenge comes in the primaries for the 2008 presidential and congressional elections when voters will have the opportunity to choose candidates committed to supporting a socially responsible trade policy and to implementing it in a worker-friendly way.

Corporate Social IRresponsibility

(From my blog, Human Rights for Workers, on February 10, 2008)

CORPORATE SOCIAL RESPONSIBILITY passed a milepost of sorts three years ago. That was when the *Economist* found that CSR had gained enough support to qualify as a movement, though one without much depth beyond the level of ideas. As the news weekly wrote in its January 22, 2005, issue, for most companies "CSR is little more than a cosmetic treatment . . . [which] goes on each morning, gets increasingly smeared by day and washes off at night." Its judgment in eighteen pages on "The Good Company" was clear: "Better that

CSR be undertaken as a cosmetic exercise than as a serious surgery to fix what doesn't need fixing . . . . It is important to resist the success of the CSR."

Well, the *Economist* has just taken a new look at that movement and finds not only that "CSR is booming" but that it "is now seen as mainstream." On balance, the thirteen-page analysis on this year's January 19 issue is more positive than negative about CSR. Indeed, some sections of the report amount to rationales for CSR, often under other labels, such as "risk management," "enlightened self-interest," and "just good business."

Perhaps the most significant finding of the report is its recognition of the fact that "the biggest problem that many companies have to deal with is something that has sprung from globalization": specifically, the risks connected with managing the global production and distribution chain that stretches across the world. Nike, with some eight hundred thousand workers in its contractor and subcontractor network, is among the firms confronted with "a challenge on a grand scale."

Why? This is the reason:

> Firms can set standards of behavior for suppliers, but they do not find it easy to enforce them. Unscrupulous suppliers may cheat, keeping two sets of records, one for show, one for real. Others, under intense pressure to keep costs low, may cut corners—allowing unpaid overtime, for example, subcontracting work to other firms that escape scrutiny . . . .
>
> Basic as it sounds, even many big companies fail to [monitor risk across the supply chain]: 60 percent of the 2,000 large companies surveyed recently . . . said they did not require suppliers to enforce a code of conduct.

A point that follows from such facts—a point that the *Economist* does not make—is that the biggest problem for global companies is also the biggest failure of CSR and its codes of conduct.

—

The *Economist* notes and applauds an attitudinal change in a growing number of firms and NGOs: it leads them to work together in formal or informal partnerships. "Both sides now see CSR as offering . . . benefits for both business and society." But does it, really? The supporting evidence is mighty skimpy.

Consider the vast resources poured into CSR activities in the past two decades, from the UN Global Compact on down. Where are the results? Results, that is, measured in changes where people work and live, rather than in the huge increase in CSR professionals on payrolls and in training. This report has amazingly little to say about problems that CSR has solved.

Could it be that CSR has actually *slowed down* progress toward solving the burgeoning problems of globalization? After all, CSR tools such as seminars and codes of conduct can, and do, lull people into complacency by creating a false impression that something real is happening—that global sweatshops are under control, that NGOs need no longer run campaigns to expose them, that the media need no longer publicize them, that public protests against them have become unnecessary.

The truth is that human progress often requires measured militancy. The civil rights movement required it. So did the women's rights movement. And so does the corporate social responsibility movement.

From my own limited contact with the corporate world, I know that there are some executives who want to do what is right and just but are, or think they are, hemmed in by the culture of their firm or industry. They themselves don't sign petitions or carry placards in demonstrations, but they need people who do. Students, ministers, workers, and others who agitate for change are the allies of a genuine movement for corporate social responsibility. Without them, CSR is an occupation expanded into a bureaucracy.

CHAPTER 19

Spatulas, Yahoo, Trade, and China

International business has changed radically in the past two decades or so, but global rules have not kept pace with those changes. The information services industry offers a prime example of that failure in China and of how one of its giants is trying to correct it. This story about my troubling experience as an Internet user was published in the August 4-11, 2008, issue of *America* magazine under the title "Buyer's Remorse" and the subtitle "Spatulas, Yahoo, and the Conscience of a Consumer."

WHEN OUR OLD WOODEN spatula showed signs of age, I looked for a replacement on my next trip to the nearby Giant Food supermarket. I found only a plastic model and was about to buy it until I read the small print: "made in China." In checking other nearby household utensils, I found that almost all came from the People's Republic.

A day or two later, I mailed a complaint to Giant's Consumer Affairs department. "Dear friends," I wrote. "It shocks me that a company of Giant Food's distinction would sell goods made in the People's Republic of China." The main point of my four-paragraph letter was to criticize the store for depending on China as a major source, even though it didn't know how the spatula or other made-in-China products were manufactured.

"Can you guarantee," I asked, "that they were not made by Protestant ministers sentenced to forced labor camps because of their religion? Or by underage children working in sweatshops? Or by college students sentenced to hard labor because they refuse to follow the dictates of the party? Or in a People's Liberation Army factory whose exports to the United States underwrite the missiles they build for firing toward Taiwan?"

The response I received did not answer my questions. Instead, the assistant director of consumer affairs wrote that over the years Giant had received many requests to boycott various products for various reasons but decided not to do so, being unwilling to make the choices for their customers. "Those who choose to boycott products made in the People's Republic of China have the right to do so," she explained, "but those who wish to purchase them ought to have that right as well."

At that time, in late 1995, I also wrote to other supermarket chains. The response from Fresh Fields was the most pointed: it said that one of Fresh Fields's founding philosophies is "to offer choices to consumers," and that therefore it was letting customers make their own choices on what to buy.

Both Giant Food and Fresh Fields were basing their position on a value held to be basic in the free market system—freedom of choice. President Bush recently expressed his belief in that value. In a speech to the U.S. Hispanic Chamber of Commerce on March 12, he warned that Congress's failure to pass more free trade agreements would deprive American families of the "choices that they've been used to." He went on: "We want our consumers to have choices when they walk into markets. The more choices available, the better it is for a consumer."

Milton and Rose Friedman laid down the rationale for that view in a ten-week PBS series on the theme "Free to Choose" in 1980 and then published a book with the same theme and title. They also compared the choices made in the supermarket to choices made in the voting booth, both seen as freedom in action.

The trouble with extolling free choice for the American shopper is that something happened to it on our way to globalization. Products made in the USA have almost disappeared from our shelves. They have been massively replaced by imports, above all by imports from China. Consumer choice for U.S.-made products is gone, or almost so.

The services sector is falling victim to the same trend. That fact hit home to me because I am a Yahoo subscriber.

Yahoo, an Internet content provider and a Web portal based in California, is a Fortune 500 multinational whose business in China is booming. In China, you do as the Chinese do. So Yahoo works closely with China's security forces in censoring the Internet. Even more serious, it is obligated to turn over to police incriminating information that has led to jail and other punishments for Chinese Yahoo users who engage in conduct the government deems unbecoming to a good citizen of China.

I am especially troubled by what has happened, for example, to Li Zhi, a thirty-two-year-old civil servant, a supporter of the China Democracy Party, who was sentenced to eight years in prison in 2003 for "inciting subversion against the state." Yahoo helped put him there. The plight of Li and two other citizens of China made the news on February 29 when they filed a lawsuit against Yahoo in a California federal court, charging that they had to endure torture, imprisonment, and other sufferings after Yahoo handed over their e-mails and other Internet information to Chinese authorities.

Yahoo—which doesn't deny working with the government—may settle the case of Li and his two co-plaintiffs out of court, as it did a similar lawsuit last November for an undisclosed sum of money. That does not end my moral dilemma. I just don't like to be connected with a company that helps a government torture people. For twelve years, I've run a Web site promoting human rights at home and abroad. At the same time, I have depended on Yahoo for its e-mail and research services.

Quitting Yahoo does not solve my problem either. As a media watchdog group, Reporters without Borders, says, Yahoo's competitors, Google, Microsoft, and Cisco Systems, all now working in China, are also following the axiom that when in China, do as the Chinese do. Under the pressure of a government equipped with armies of informers and the latest in surveillance technology, the Internet companies have agreed to censor their search engines to filter material overcritical of authorities. "This makes the regime's job very much easier because these firms are the main entry points to the Internet," Reporters without Borders says, "If a Web site is not listed by their search engines, material posted on them has about as much chance of being found as a message in a bottle thrown into the sea."

I may find I can switch from Yahoo to a comparable provider not in China. That would get me personally off the hook in this instance, but it would change nothing else.

Fortunately, another California-based Fortune 500 multinational with a booming business in China, Google, is searching for a solution. Making money on information services while at the same time collaborating with a government to suppress information and having a congressman call two Google executives moral pygmies at a public hearing last year—all that is not a comfortable position to be in. Google wants U.S. government help to get out of it. Under a corporate philosophy that proclaims "you can make money without doing evil," Google is exploring an approach not tried before. This initiative relies on the logic of international trade law, which, in principle, outlaws barriers to trade. Since government censorship of information is a serious trade barrier for American companies in China, it follows that China's barrier should be outlawed as such through U.S. bilateral and multilateral trade agreements.

Timothy Wu, associate professor of law at Columbia University and a scholar on telecommunications and trade law, came to the same conclusion on his own: that China's Internet censorship violates international trade law. In a paper on "The World Trade Law of Internet Filtering," he emphasizes the cross-border character of Internet services: "Much of Internet can be reached from anywhere, making nearly everyone on the Internet a potential importer or exporter of services (and sometimes goods)."

In China's case, Dr. Wu contends, the government agreed to reform the protectionist practices of PRC firms in the services sector as a condition of entry into the World Trade Organization in late 2001. Instead, however, China has become one of the "world's more active filterers of Internet services." He regards China as probably in conflict with one of the key WTO pacts—the little known General Agreement on Trade in Services or GATS. The twenty-first-century expansion of the Internet, he insists, has "leaped beyond what was contemplated in GATS or subsequent telecommunications agreements, . . . [and] requires new thinking about how barriers come about."

A West Coast advocacy group, the California First Amendment Coalition, is contributing some new thinking. In an oral and written case to U.S. trade officials, the coalition specifically identifies a WTO and GATS principle that China is violating—"national treatment." Basic in all trade agreements, this principle requires a country to treat imported goods and services the same as those produced locally. But China uses "a wide range of laws and regulations that result in de jure or de facto" discriminatory treatment of U.S. companies, according to the Coalition's paper, and is thereby actively restricting the operations of U.S. Internet companies "while at the same time promoting Chinese Internet companies in the same or similar activities."

At a hearing on May 20 of the Senate judiciary subcommittee on human rights and the law, Nicole Wong, Google's deputy general counsel, repeated the company position that the U.S. government should make combating Internet censorship a top priority. "It is vital," she said, "for the U.S. Departments of State and Commerce and the Office of the U.S. Trade Representative—in this and in future administrations—to make censorship a central element of our bilateral and multilateral [trade] agendas."

U.S. government officials, however, have yet to embrace this precedent-setting approach. After all, the plight of the Internet giants in China is not unique. Other global industries also must live under trade policies that have not caught up with the twenty-first century. Multinational corporations still operate under rules of the world trade and investment system that was patched together in the four decades after the end of World War II.

Under the principles laid down by leaders who established the WTO, all its member nations (now 152) are equal and have the same rights in the international marketplace. Dictatorships and autocratic governments enjoy the same rights and privileges as democratic ones. And so China, exploiting its own opportunistic blend of Vladimir Lenin and Adam Smith, naturally takes full advantage of a position of unfreedom at home—especially its heavily controlled labor force—to mass produce for free markets abroad, especially for the largest free market in the world.

Result: last year the United States imported $321,442,900,000 worth of goods from China, a record sure to be broken again in 2008. Constrained by space, the print media publish those figures only in abbreviated form, if they publish them at all, by using a tiny *b* to replace the final six digits, thus obscuring the 321,442,900,000 dollar votes we cast for unfreedom.

In a 2001 policy paper for the UNDP on "The Global Governance of Trade as if Development Really Mattered," Dani Rodrik, professor of international political economy at Harvard, proposed that a reformed trade system include this principle: "Nondemocratic countries cannot count on the same trade privileges as democratic ones." The idea did not catch on in 2001, and hasn't since then.

It does not seem to stand a chance, above all because now that China is in the WTO, Beijing can veto any reform that would diminish the advantages it now enjoys. Nevertheless, a broad range of ideas ought to be on the table for a serious trade policy review in light of the need to replace the president's Trade Promotion Authority law, which expired last July. To prepare for that review and the actions that should follow, Congress would be wise to commission an economist like Rodrik to prepare a report on "The Global Governance of Trade as if Human Rights Really Mattered."

CHAPTER 20

Personal Responsibility

The word *social* has many different meanings. When used as a qualifier in the expression *social responsibility*, it can imply that the responsibility is society's, not mine or yours, never a personal one. But personal and social responsibilities are intertwined. In fact, correctly understood, social responsibility is a personal responsibility. This book, and this chapter in particular, seeks to put across that point, starting with the first article below, which appeared in the April 2007 issue of *U.S. Catholic* magazine under the title "Don't Shop till They Drop," followed by five shorter articles from Human Rights for Workers.

I DON'T SHOP at Wal-Mart. I don't wear Nike sneakers or any product with a Nike swoosh. I avoid buying anything made in China.

Until fairly late in life, I didn't really care where things came from. I didn't examine labels to see where clothing was manufactured or scan the copyright page of books to see where they were printed. If I liked a product, liked the price, and needed it for myself or the family, I bought it. No hesitation. But I've changed.

—

Now I have a visceral reaction against buying a sweatshirt that might be made by a ten-year-old girl or a shoe that might be made by a priest or a Falun Gong member locked up in China's notorious forced labor camps. What changed me?

About fifteen years ago, during a job-related trip to Bangladesh, I saw little girls and boys as young as ten or eleven toiling for a few cents an hour in factories assembling garments for Wal-Mart and other stores in the United States and Europe. The sight affected me deeply. Back home, I attended a meeting of a Washington, D.C., group called the Child Labor Coalition and choked up when I reported on what I saw in Bangladesh.

My personal experience in visiting factories in Bangladesh, and later in other Asian countries, opened my eyes. Besides continuing to support the Child Labor Coalition, I started to monitor the fate of workers more closely by launching a Web site, Human Rights for Workers. Believe me, the size of the scandal is beyond belief. The labor problems of Wal-Mart and Nike as world leaders in their particular domains are only symbols of the much wider problems in the globalized network of production and supply chains where sweatshops flourish. This network serves some seven hundred thousand multinational firms with products from factories they do not own, made by 70,000,000 workers (mostly women) they don't employ.

And U.S. workers aren't immune to the effects of this network. With cheaper labor abroad, the United States has lost millions of decently paid manufacturing jobs—2,800,000 since 2001, according to the AFL-CIO. Also, the service industry jobs that have replaced many of these manufacturing jobs do not pay enough for people to live with dignity in the United States.

Most people are shocked when they learn about a new sweatshop scandal—say, a Hanes factory in Bangladesh employing two hundred underage boys and girls at wages as low as six and a half *cents* an hour—but they should be equally shocked when they learn about children in the United States who have grown up malnourished and in poor health because their parents earn only poverty-level wages on full-time jobs without health insurance. Realistically, what can you—a shocked you—do to correct such gross violations of human rights?

You have a surprising number of choices. You can boycott a product made in a sweatshop, if you know the name of the product, or its retail outlet. You can write a letter of concern to the embassy of the country where the tragedy occurred. You can make a donation to a worker rights advocacy organization, such as the Child Labor Coalition.

And you can help on the home front. Yes, here in the richest country in the world, we have our own brand of sweatshops and near sweatshops—in restaurants, in meat-packing plants, in clothing factories, in hospitals, in farm fields, even on university campuses—where grown men and women work full time at near-starvation wages. You are needed to end that national scandal

As a Catholic who has witnessed violations of human rights overseas, I personally cannot support companies that I know profit off poor workers there or here—and many do both. But there are other, often more effective, ways to get involved. You can do so, for example, by lobbying and voting for raising the minimum wage at the federal level and in your own state and local community. And you can become an active participant in a grassroots campaign.

Many ordinary Americans, God bless them, are already involved in such local campaigns, which have done much better than Congress in increasing the pay of millions of underpaid workers in communities across the United States. In fact, thanks to such campaigns, at least half of all working men and women in the United States now live in cities and states where the official minimum pay rate is higher than the decade-old federal minimum of $5.15 an hour (soon to become $7.25).

There are now countless churches, community organizations, labor unions, and other local advocacy groups taking up the cause of the poor. In fact, their campaigns constitute a grassroots living-wage movement that policymakers can no longer ignore.

How to locate current campaigns and future ones? The best national source is the Living Wage Resource Center in Washington,

D.C. On this organization's Web site, at www.livingwagecampaign. org, you'll also find how-to-do-it information and useful links to other sources. For local information, check your parish, civic organizations, labor unions, and newspapers.

But even while Congress is currently attempting to increase the minimum wage, this movement does not want to settle for a *minimum* wage. After all, for a worker employed fifty-two weeks of the year, the $7.50-an-hour state minimum established in California in 2005 comes to only $15,600 a year, which is $3,750 below the 2005 federal poverty level for a typical family of four. The real goal is to win a *living* wage, or *just* wage in Catholic social teaching, one adequate to support a worker and his family at a decent level. There is no formula for setting that level for every community since the cost of living and other circumstances vary geographically. Arriving at a fair amount in your area requires much bargaining. That's why justice-minded men and women need to participate in the negotiating process to press for a dollar amount above the barest minimum.

The negotiations may appear to be only about money but don't forget that a basic moral value is at stake. Catholic teaching regards a living wage as a matter of justice. So the Catechism states, "A just wage is the legitimate fruit of work. To refuse or withhold it can be a grave injustice." Or as Pope Leo XIII put it more than a century ago in his historic encyclical *On the Condition of Labor* (*Rerum Novarum*), "To defraud anyone of wages that are his due is a crime which rises to the avenging anger of Heaven."

During a campaign to raise the minimum wage of Santa Fe, Father Jerome Martinez, a downtown pastor who supported the cause, was asked why he didn't stick to religion. "Well, pardon me—this is religion," he later told a reporter. "The Scripture is full of matters of justice. How can you worship a God that you do not see and then oppress the workers that you do see?"

After much controversy, the city of Santa Fe raised its minimum gradually from $5.15 an hour to the current level, $9.50, the highest rate in the United States. The winning argument was quite straightforward: "It's just immoral to pay $5.15; they can't live on that."

But is pay justice economically feasible? No, according to opponents who argue that raising minimum wages actually destroys jobs. But recent empirical research by economists refutes that contention. It shows that adopting higher minimum pay has not stunted employment and, in some instances, has even increased it. Moreover, in a joint statement issued last October, 650 economists—including six Nobel Prize winners in economics—asserted that a modest, inflation-indexed increase in the minimum wage, at both the national and state levels, "can significantly improve the lives of low-income workers and their families without the adverse effects that critics have claimed."

The very idea of having government set a wage floor offends some people. But Responsible Wealth, a national network of business people, investors, and affluent, holds that "paying employees a living wage is good business, creating stronger communities and better customers," and urges business to sign a "covenant" in support of that goal.

From my own perspective, reached after long personal strivings to apply Catholic social teaching to modern problems, I find much virtue in this movement for a living wage. I see more and more ordinary citizens, working together, living up to the words of the Gospel to love our neighbor. I see them disproving the immoral theory that human lives can improve only through value-free market competition. I see them showing how people can address other modern challenges, such as world poverty and unjust international trade and investment laws. In short, I see people moving toward a world in which thy will is done on earth as it is in heaven.

> The article above has a serious omission that I spotted too late. I was struggling to squeeze too much material into a short article about living wage campaigns. Still, I should not have neglected to point out that unions and collective bargaining are the best means to gain and keep decent wages and working conditions and that citizens should respond to calls to support organizing campaigns.

The Holocaust as Lenten Reading

(This personal examination of conscience first appeared in the March 11, 1998, issue of Human Rights for Workers.)

DURING LENT THIS month, I again thumbed through my copy of Daniel Jonah Goldhagen's powerful book, *Hitler's Willing Executioners: Ordinary Germans and the Holocaust.* Reflecting on the Holocaust is, for me, a profound spiritual exercise.

After all, as the son of an ethnic German father born near the borders of present-day Austria, I might have lived through the Nazi era in Germany. Instead of listening to anti-Jewish views in my home in Chicago (as I did as a teenager), I might have acted on them in Berlin or Nuremberg. Instead of serving in the U.S. Army during World War II, I might have served in Hitler's army or one of Germany's murderous police units. So I can't help wondering:

Would I have been among the multitudes of Germans, young and old, who (as you can still see in TV documentaries) marched in Nazi parades and saluted in Hitler rallies? No, I tell myself.

Would I have played a role in the extermination of Jews? No, I tell myself. No, I would not have beaten Jewish neighbors or shot Jewish men, women, and children in the back or herded them into death camps. No.

But would I have done anything, anything at all, to stop the carnage? Even if I would not have joined in what Germans high and low did against Jews, would I have raised my voice against the atrocities? On that I am . . . not sure.

I am shaken by that thought—the possibility that I might have remained mute amid the barbarities committed by people high and low in Nazi Germany. My fear stems from an honest self-appraisal. I remember the many occasions when I, as an American living in freedom, have remained silent, done nothing, about obvious injustices. And that passivity was under circumstances when the cost of doing something, showing some courage, was mighty small—nothing compared to what it was for people living under

—

the Third Reich, and still is for those living in the People's Republic of China.

A Physician Asks: What Would I Have Done?

This physician's visit to the Holocaust Museum, described here in an article from the October 2, 2004, issue of Human Rights for Workers, has insights into the challenge of exercising personal responsibility in one's occupation.

As a physician dedicated to the ethical principles of his profession, Dr. Sherwin B. Nuland always felt certain that if he had been practicing in Germany during the Third Reich, he would in no way have cooperated with the Nazi regime in carrying out the Holocaust. That was his assumption before a recent visit to the U.S. Holocaust Museum in Washington, D.C. Now he is not so sure.

Nuland calls the Holocaust Museum "a place to learn, to look within oneself, and to ponder the nature of our humanity," and he holds that especially true for the museum's special exhibition on Deadly Medicine: Creating the Master Race. There his own pondering led him to imagine himself as someone in the German medical establishment during the 1930s and 1940s. His self-examination was not reassuring. It shook him deeply. "To my startled dismay," he writes in a magazine article, "I found myself understanding why much of the German medical establishment acted as it did. I realized that, given the circumstances, I might have done the same."

His explanation takes eight pages of the *New Republic*'s September 13/20 issue. Like the Deadly Medicine exhibit, Nuland traces the dedication of international eugenics movement to improving the "purity of the human race by better breeding." It was so successful in Germany that "who but a few visionaries would see any danger in the promotion of purity?"

"It is hardly surprises that National Socialism in Germany would embrace the concept of eugenics," he observes, and painfully recounts how Hitler and his regime expanded the concept step-by-step toward the Final Solution, the program of "ridding Germany and eventually Europe of the pestilential disease of Judaism."

Nuland dwells on the shocking truth that his own medical profession cooperated in Hitler's program of a *Judenfrei* Europe. "Physicians again and again participated in ways that were as murderous as though they had themselves been officers in Himmler's SS (as in fact so many of them were)," he points out. "Among [those ways] was the eugenically justified euthanasia program that was the forerunner of the gas chambers."

How could the medical profession so degrade itself? One reason he gives is this: "The German medical establishment was heir to a grand tradition of accomplishment and international respect. When it took on eugenics as a worthy goal, it was convinced of the righteousness of its intent. Even when some of its own members began to voice concerns about the direction which the research and its application were going, many authoritative voices drowned out the relatively few protests."

In other words, professional arrogance and a reluctance to question collective policy dominated the culture. "No association or guild," Nuland writes, "was more complicit in the rise of Nazism and the desecration committed by its leaders and followers than the profession of medicine, in the form both of its organizations and its individual members. This needs to be more widely known, and not only by today's doctors. In our shame, great lessons are to be learned."

From the imprimatur that medical science in the United States, Britain, and Germany gave to eugenics and the tragic consequences in Europe, Nuland draws this lesson: the importance of recognizing that "scientific enterprise" has limitations. He insists that scientific findings arise in a setting that is political and social. "Not only that, but its directions and even its conclusions are influenced by the personal motivations, needs, and strivings of those who practice it, some of which may not be apparent to these men and women themselves. The danger in this lies . . . in the inability of society and the community of scientists to recognize the pervading influence of such an unpalatable reality, which flies in the face of the claims [of detached objectivity] that form the groundwork for our worship of the scientific enterprise."

> Dr. Nuland teaches surgery and the history of medicine at Yale and is the author of *How We Die* and *Doctors: the Biography of Medicine*, among other books. His *New Republic* article, "The Death of Hippocrates: When Medicine Turns Evil," is worth reading not only as a reminder of the Holocaust's horrors but also as a model of self-reflection, useful for persons in other professions and occupations.

Which Way to Go, Mr. CEO?

(From the January 5, 2004, issue of Human Rights for Workers)

LET'S SAY YOU are a top management official at Wal-Mart, Nike, or some other major American corporation, and you are deciding the future direction of your business. In recent years you have come to rely on workers in the People's Republic of China to make a large part of your company's goods and profits. You used to deny that your products are made in sweatshops, but you now know that the on-site evidence is undeniable. You face increasing pressures to make your company "socially responsible."

So what to do? You seek guidance from lawyers and other experts. At root, however, the choices you face are two, exemplified by the opposing approaches carefully delineated by two world figures. Here is one approach, capsulized in this quotation:

> In [a free] economy, there is one and only one social responsibility of business—to use its resources and engage in activities designed to increase profits so long as it stays within the rules of the game, which is to say, engages in open and free competition, without deception or fraud. Few trends could so thoroughly undermine the very foundation of our free society as the acceptance by

corporate officials of a social responsibility other than *to make as much money for their stockholders as possible.*

> —Milton Friedman, the distinguished professor of economics, writing in his best-selling book *Capitalism and Freedom* (p. 133; emphasis added)

I call this the *not-to-worry* approach. It can be very comforting to sweatshop-plagued corporate leaders. It tells them, on the authority of an eminent economist who is a Nobel Prize winner, that in dedicating yourself to making as much money as possible for your stockholders, you are doing the right thing and also fighting to keep our society free.

Then, there's another approach, capsulized in these three propositions:

1. "There exist acts which per se and in themselves, independently of circumstances, are always seriously wrong" (that is, prohibited because they are "always and without exception intrinsically evil" [emphasis in original]).
2. Among such evils are "degrading conditions of work, which treat laborers as mere instruments of profit."
3. "So long as [such evils] infect human civilization they contaminate those who inflict them more than those who suffer them"

> —Pope John Paul II in his encyclical letter *Veritatis Splendor* (para. 80)

I call this the *you'd-**better**-worry* approach. It prohibits treating workers as mere instruments of profit. Morally, it places a severe limitation on you even if the existing rules of the game do not.

It's your choice, Mr. CEO. Which approach will you take?

A Graduation Pledge

(This updates a note that appeared in the January 12, 1998, issue of Human Rights for Workers.)

"I PLEDGE TO explore and take into account the social and environmental consequences of any job I consider and will try to improve these aspects of any organizations for which I work." So reads a pledge taken each year by students at more than a hundred colleges and universities each year. The voluntary commitment leaves students free to determine for themselves what they consider to be socially and environmentally responsible. At many schools, the pledge is part of graduation ceremonies.

The idea for the pledge originated at Humboldt State University in Arcata, California, in 1987. Manchester College in North Manchester, Indiana, coordinates a national campaign called the Graduation Pledge Alliance, with a Web site of its own (www. graduationpledge.org).

The Kid Sister Test

(From the September 21, 1998, issue of Human Rights for Workers)

How CAN YOU tell whether your workplace is ripe for a sexual harassment lawsuit? Interpreting the relevant laws and court decisions can be confusing. Applying them is even more so. Ronald M. Green, a New York lawyer, suggests taking a more basic approach—applying what he calls the "kid sister test."

It works this way. Imagine that your kid sister (or a teenage daughter) gets a job in your office. "How does that make you feel?" Green asks and continues, "Would you want someone you care deeply about hearing what you hear, seeing what you see, walking where you walk, knowing what you know about others in the office?"

Green, who represents management in employment law matters, says it has been his own experience that many corporations fail that basic test. Writing recently in the Sunday business section of the *New York Times,* he explained, "Offensive behavior in the typical workplace ranges from the explicit to the subtle. Pornographic magazines and X-rated pictures on the Web and via e-mail fill office monitors and desks. Office banter about Viagra spawns full-scale, open-air discussions. Are these situations you would want your kid sister to experience? I would suggest that if you are in any way uncomfortable, it's time to start changing the environment."

You can apply the same test beyond your own immediate workplace. Imagine young females of your kid sister's age working in a sweatshop producing clothes, toys, or some other goods for your home. Offensive behavior in the typical sweatshop ranges from mild verbal abuse to physical punishment, including various forms of sexual harassment. Offensive working conditions range from excessively long hours (six or seven days a week, with no vacations) to exposure to deadly fumes.

Are these the kind of situations you would want someone resembling your kid sister to experience? Especially someone who, in a distant sweatshop, is working to make products for you and yours? If you are in any way uncomfortable with this grim reality, it's time to start changing the environment.

It's easier, of course, to change the environment in your own workplace. The law is on your side. But as the global economy multiplies the number of women working for you in other lands, it's time also to get international law on your side. That won't happen without support from you and others like you.

Chapter 21

The Global Compact

(From the February 8, 1999, issue of Human Rights for Workers)

WAS HE DREAMING, or what?

Kofi Annan, United Nations secretary-general, issued an unusual challenge to international big business at the late January (1999) annual meeting of the World Economic Forum in Davos, Switzerland. There, amid one thousand top executives of corporations with revenues of at least $1 billion a year, Annan urged businessmen and women to work with the UN and UN agencies to promote "a set of core values in the areas of human rights, labor standards, and environmental standards" in the global economy.

"I propose," he continued, "that you, the business leaders gathered in Davos, and we, the United Nations, initiate a global compact of shared values and principles, which will give a human face to the global market."

He went on to be specific about the "great opportunities and great responsibilities" facing corporate leaders in promoting worker rights. For example:

> Don't wait for every country to introduce laws protecting freedom of association and the right to collective

bargaining. You can at least make sure your own employees and, those of your subcontractors, enjoy those rights. You can at least make sure that you yourselves are not employing underage children or forced labor, either directly or indirectly. And you can make sure that, in your own hiring and firing policies, you do not discriminate on grounds of race, creed, gender, or ethnic origin.

Failure to take steps to give the global economy a "human face," he said, will leave it "fragile and vulnerable—vulnerable to backlash from all the 'isms' of our post-cold-war world: protectionism, populism, nationalism, ethnic chauvinism, fanaticism, and terrorism."

He reminded his audience that "the global markets and multilateral trading system we have today" happened not by accident, but by the "enlightened policy choices made by governments since 1945." To preserve the global economy into the twenty-first century, he argued, "all of us—governments, corporations, nongovernmental organizations, international organizations—have to make the right choices now."

Note that Annan puts corporations right after governments on that list. Perhaps he should put them first. Most political leaders today, whatever their party or personal beliefs, are so dependent on corporate campaign funds that they seldom take any initiative that doesn't get a significant green light from the corporate world.

Annan told the corporate executives that "we have to choose between a global market driven only by calculations of short-term profit and one which has a human face . . . between a selfish free-for-all in which we ignore the fate of the losers and *a future in which the strong and successful accept their responsibilities, showing global vision and leadership*" (my emphasis).

As I have pointed out in these pages, progress in the global struggle for worker rights is stymied by the opposition of powerful business groups, and a breakthrough is very unlikely without some responsible leadership from the employers' side. I even suggested that from the logic of Nike's own code of conduct, which says, "We are driven to do not only what is required but what is expected of a leader," Nike's own CEO, Phil Knight, ought to step into that role.

Was I dreaming or what?

Three sentences in Kofi Annan's address at Davos greatly watered down his proposal:

> There is enormous pressure from various interest groups to load the trade regime and investment agreements with restrictions aimed at preserving standards in the three areas I have mentioned [human rights, labor, and the environment]. These are legitimate concerns. But restrictions on trade and investment are not the right means to use when tackling them.

Instead, the UN secretary-general favors finding "a way to achieve our proclaimed standards by other means." Fat chance. Purely voluntary means won't work. They don't in any other important problem area—from drunken driving on up to international piracy of Hollywood movies. It is naive to think otherwise.

Promoting the "Work of God"

(From the October 8, 1999, issue of Human Rights for Workers)

I NEVER THOUGHT that I'd hear such ideas discussed in the headquarters of the U.S. Chamber of Commerce. But there I was, in the chamber's Anheuser-Busch Briefing Center, listening to the following:

> The Reverend Leon H. Sullivan, author of the Sullivan Principles for companies in South Africa under apartheid, saying that he, along with UN Secretary-General Kofi Annan, would soon announce the Global Sullivan

Principles, designed to cover corporations in the global economy.

The president of the American Apparel Manufacturers Association, Larry Martin, describing a global initiative to eliminate sweatshops, with a code of conduct and a certification program supported by apparel manufacturers in Africa, Asia, Central America, and the Caribbean.

The executive vice president of Business for Social Responsibility, Marjorie Chorlins, stating that the elements of "what makes a good business decision is shifting" and now involves working toward "a more just society."

The setting was the chamber's October 6 conference on Corporate Responsibility and Globalization. Its purpose, said L. Craig Johnstone, senior vice president of international economic and national security affairs, was to celebrate corporate achievements and to examine "how we can do better."

Among nearly a dozen speakers in the morning session, Sullivan was by far the most hard-hitting. He gave a preview of what he called the new Sullivan Principles, a charter designed to "help companies to put their houses in order" in the global economy. The principles are "simple, direct, so a child could memorize them," he said and would apply from Mobile, Alabama, to Peking, China. Among other things, it would ban child labor and guarantee the right of workers to organize.

"This is the work of God," Sullivan intoned, speaking as the preacher that he is. "My name must not be associated with a fake," he said. The initiative would rely on "the carrot rather than the hammer." But he added if the carrot does not produce results, "I will still have a hammer," which he suggested would involve disinvestment campaigns if necessary.

I stayed only for the first half of an all-day conference, long enough to sense that some chamber leaders are exploring a new direction for the corporate world. Not long ago, the chamber hierarchy held the very notion of corporate codes of conduct as illicit. A business friend of mine was once severely castigated for openly supporting codes.

Will this be a windblown change of direction or a change of heart? Maybe it doesn't matter, just as long as it happens. Reverend Sullivan seems dedicated to make it so.

> Before leaving the chamber's conference, I signed a list of participants interested in being kept informed on developments. That led to my getting a letter soon thereafter from Leon Sullivan inviting me to attend a "historic event" at UN headquarters. On November 2, Secretary-General Kofi Annan and the Reverend Sullivan would make an official announcement on the Global Sullivan Principles, which, the letter assured me, "are in keeping with the Global Compact" that Kofi Annan had earlier announced in Davos. Unfortunately, I didn't attend this event. In any case, it took another eight months of discussions and negotiations before the UN Global Compact was ready for its public debut, which I describe in the following article.

Compact Consummated

(From the August 1, 2000, issue of Human Rights for Workers)

"THE PROBLEM IS this," Kofi Annan, secretary-general of the United Nations, told one thousand corporate chieftains at the Swiss mountain resort of Davos in January 1999. "The spread of markets outpaces the ability of societies and their political systems to adjust to them, let alone to guide the course they take." To help guide that course, he urged business leaders to join a "creative partnership" with the UN to promote "a set of core values in the areas of human rights, labor standards, and environmental standards" in the global economy.

At the UN headquarters on July 26, the CEOs of nearly fifty multinational corporations responded by signing a "global compact" to respect human rights, labor standards, and environmental standards in their business operations. Of the compact's nine general principles, four involve labor standards, which include upholding "freedom of association and the effective recognition of the right to collective bargaining."

The labor standard's principles are drawn word for word from the International Labor Organization's Declaration on Fundamental Principles and Rights at Work, adopted with the unanimous support of employer representatives at the ILO Conference in June 1998. The other principles come from the UN Universal Declaration of Human Rights and the Rio Principles on Environment and Development.

ILO Declaration on Rights at Work

[A]ll Members, even if they have not ratified the Conventions in question, have an obligation arising from the very fact of membership in the [International Labor] Organization to respect, to promote and to realize, in good faith and in accordance with the Constitution, the principles concerning the fundamental rights which are the subject of those Conventions, namely:

(a) freedom of association and the effective recognition of the right to collective bargaining;

(b) the elimination of all forms of forced or compulsory labor;

(c) the effective abolition of child labor; and

(d) the elimination of discrimination in respect of employment and occupation.

—*Article 2 of the ILO Declaration on Fundamental Principles and Rights at Work adopted by the International Labor Conference in Geneva on June 18, 1998.*

John Evans, general secretary of the Trade Union Advisory Committee of the Paris-based Organisation of Economic Co-operation and Development (OECD), led a three-man international trade union delegation that attended the high-level UN meeting. Afterward, the delegation had these comments: "The UN Global Compact offers a further opportunity for global dialogue between enterprises, trade unions, and nongovernmental organizations. In so doing, it fulfills a critical need, but it must not usurp the role of binding rules to regulate the behavior of multinational companies."

Annan said the UN would establish a Global Compact office to "finalize a priority plan for collaborative action." But there will be no monitoring of how the business partners—which include Bayer, BPAmoco, Dupont, Ericsson, Nike, and Unilever—comply with the terms of the Compact.

In a letter to Kofi Annan, a group of nineteen human rights and environmental activists last month criticized the Global Compact for its lack of monitoring and enforcement provisions and proposed an alternative—a Citizens Compact that stresses the need of "a legal framework for corporate behavior in the global economy." They wrote:

> We are well aware that many corporations would like nothing better than to wrap themselves in the flag of the United Nations to 'bluewash' their public image while at the same time avoiding significant changes to their behavior . . . Asking corporations, many of which are repeat offenders of both the law and commonly accepted standards of responsibility, to endorse a vague statement . . . draws attention away from the need for more substantial action to hold corporations accountable for their behavior.

What will the Global Compact matter to the men and women who work for us in Asia, the Caribbean, and Latin America? There are so many millions of them employed producing for the American market that they are de facto members of the U.S. labor force.

The supreme test of the Global Compact is what effect it will have on the immense labor force of ours in China, which is bound to expand once China enters the World Trade Organization. Will it make any difference to the many women in China's sweatshops? Will it, for example, ensure the payment of a decent wage? But the Global Compact's principles say nothing about wages. Neither, oddly, do the ILO's Fundamental Principles.

Both the ILO and the Global Compact principles, however, are fairly explicit about freedom of association and the right of collective bargaining. That's a challenge to the many Global Compact corporate partners who have business operations in China. China is the world's ideal "union-free" environment. Employers there don't have to intimidate or fire union organizers. The government's security police does that for them. "Troublemakers" are locked up in labor reeducation camps. The party units that operate in workplaces maintain discipline in-house.

Kofi Annan says that a company operating in a country that does not allow unions should permit its workers to organize and bargain. Nice idea, but naive, unless the UN can work a miracle. Most U.S. multinationals are notorious for opposing unionization, by fair means or foul, in the United States, Malaysia, and other countries where unionization is legally permitted. Why would they embrace unions where they are *prohibited?*

Corporate cooperation is absolutely necessary to succeed in wiping out sweatshops and guaranteeing worker rights. Kofi Annan is right about that. But it will take more than the current design of the Global Compact to change the antiunionism that pervades modern corporate culture. The first to step is to recognize two realities:

> An anonymous White House staffer told a Time magazine reporter a few years ago: "The fact is that nothing we can do short of war can significantly impact on what China does to its own people. Meanwhile, we want a piece of the pie, a big piece, and we aim to get it." The November 29, 1993, article in which that quote appeared was titled "Putting Business First." Public rhetoric is different; foreign trade

and investment are now portrayed as promoting freedom. But the reality is that narrow commercialism still drives the way multinationals handle themselves in China and the way the U.S. government shapes its China policy.

As part of its policies, China has granted foreigners rights that they have not enjoyed since the colonial era. American and other foreign business have the freedom to form chambers of commerce and other organizations to advance their common interests. But China's workers are by force prohibited from doing the same thing. Foreign business leaders also have the right to petition the government at local and national levels of the People's Republic. But China's citizens are jailed for doing the same thing. That kind of dichotomy, as Wei Jingsheng once warned, cannot endure. Nor should the UN tolerate it.

The UN Global Compact laid the groundwork for a more ambitious UN endeavor to integrate human rights into the global economy. It wasn't planned that way. See the next chapter for an account of how that happened. A Harvard professor, John Ruggie, a coarchitect of the Global Compact, is the central figure in the new UN initiative to universalize the UN Declaration of Human Rights.

CHAPTER 22

Business and Human Rights

The United Nations is involved as never before in trying to embed human rights in the policies and practices of global business. I have followed and reported on this new project from its 2003 origins through its evolution into a promising paradigm for multinational corporations in the twenty-first century. A shorter and different version of this chapter appeared in the December 1, 2008, issue of *America* under the title "Big Business and the UN."

As I BROWSED the Web one winter morning, a dispute at the United Nations caught my eye. Disputes are nothing special at the UN, but this one was right down my alley. It dealt with human rights and multinational corporations (or transnational corporations in non-American English). The controversy centered on whether the UN should take a more active role in advancing human rights in the global economy. Specifically, it focused on whether the UN Council on Human Rights should adopt a document titled "Norms on the Responsibilities of Transnational Corporations and Other Business Enterprises with Regard to Human Rrights," or Norms for short.

That seven-page document, a compilation of human rights standards from thirty-six UN treaties, conventions, and other international policy instruments, became extremely controversial when a subsidiary unit of the council (then called a commission) adopted it in August 2003. I first learned about it from a letter attacking it in the *Financial Times* and from a sharp rebuttal in the same pages just two days later at the end of 2003. After downloading the document on New Year's Day 2004, I wrote a short analysis titled "Global Norms Put Heat on Business" and published it in the January 6, 2004, issue of my Web site, Human Rights for Workers.

So began my involvement, as a writer and advocate, in a dramatic story that continues to this day. Thanks to the Internet, I have managed to follow the fight closely, even though I didn't write up every round.

Taking the lead among the opponents from the very start was the U.S. Council of International Business, whose membership of over three hundred U.S.-based multinationals makes it influential in world affairs. In his December 17, 2003, *Financial Times* letter, Thomas M. T. Niles, then president of the council, objected to the Norms because, if approved, they would "create a new international legal framework [making corporations] responsible for implementing international treaties and conventions." Besides, the Norms are unnecessary because, he claimed, most companies are already taking human rights seriously.

Two days later, the *Financial Times* published a letter from a Norms supporter, Mary Robinson, executive director of the Ethical Globalization Initiative and former UN High Commissioner for Human Rights. Many corporations are indeed committed to respecting human rights, she wrote, but most are not. She saw hope in the fact that seven large companies had already started using the Norms to guide their own activities—forerunners of many more corporations that she expected to be using them "when making decisions about their operating methods, personnel policies, procurement, and investment decisions."

That's a summary of how my 2004 Web report summarized the opposing positions. But I didn't leave it at that. I went on to volunteer my own advice to the U.S. Business Council on "Why to Take the High Ground." Here are two points I made:

> Governments actively protect the rights and interests of business not only through domestic legislation but more and more through a network of international law and intergovernmental organizations. But there is a huge void in international safeguards that protect the rights and interests of labor. As global integration intensifies and global communications increase, that void becomes more and more difficult to ignore and more and more difficult to justify.

> Don't underestimate Mrs. Mary Robinson and the power of the idea she is promoting. Business's heavy dependence on the protection of international law and intergovernmental organizations while vigorously opposing those benefits to others is increasingly being recognized as selfish, unbalanced, unfair, and untenable.

In writing that article four years ago, I felt that a significant chapter could be beginning in the history of globalization. I saw corporations, human rights groups, and other "stakeholders" in the global economy becoming engaged in a joint initiative to bring law and order to a large area of the world where it is much in deficit. Spurred by that conviction, I wrote fifteen more reports about that initiative for my Web site and Weblog during the next four years. I doggedly followed up with two separate op-ed articles, neither of which broke into the pages of the *New York Times,* the *Washington Post,* or the *Boston Globe.* It took a certain amount of doggedness to pursue a story that the U.S. media ignored even in its news pages.

Of course, the media love controversies, but this one, no matter how great its potential for real-world change might be, is highly abstract and without gripping visuals. It has to compete against big stories about two wars, the ups and downs of the stock market, campaigns for political office, rising gas prices, and other momentous events that generate a surplus of visuals. There is a parallel competition in assigning priorities within the overall struggle for human rights itself, as illustrated by where I placed the "Global Norms Put Heat on Business" article on my Web site. In hindsight, I think it should have led off that January 6, 2004, issue. Instead, I placed it fourth. The first article in that issue, "More on Wage-Cheating in China," exposed the scandal that millions of workers in China's export industries had been paid at rates below the legally required minimum and that employers were ignoring the demands of justice to make restitution. That was an important issue at the time. And it still is. But it's also typical of stories I have had to ignore as I focused on the reform of U.S. trade policy and the aftermath of the Norms controversy.

The Norms controversy became so polarized that in July of 2005 UN Secretary-General Kofi Annan, in accordance with a formal request by the Human Rights Commission, appointed his own special representative on human rights and business, John G. Ruggie, professor of international affairs at Harvard University's Kennedy School of Government and a former UN assistant secretary-general under Annan. When Ruggie arrived in Geneva a short time later, the diplomatic representative of a member country told him: "We've had a train-wreck. Please get the train back on track." The odds of succeeding seemed mighty small at the time.

Yet three years later, the train was not only back on track but moving forward with a visionary Harvard professor at the throttle. In June 2008 the forty-seven-member Human Rights Council settled any lingering question about UN involvement with a clear signal: *full speed ahead.* It gave unanimous approval both to Ruggie's strategic policy plan for that involvement and to a new three-year mandate for Ruggie to carry it out.

Ruggie described his plan in detail in his council report titled "Protect, Respect, and Remedy: A Framework for Business and Human Rights." That "framework," hammered out with concerned groups, especially with business, amounts to a human rights paradigm for corporations operating in the highly globalized twenty-first century. Thereby it added another dimension to the

December 2008 celebration of the sixtieth anniversary of the Universal Declaration of Human Rights.

Ruggie's four years (1997-2001) as UN assistant secretary-general for strategic planning under Annan, and another four years (2001 to 2005) as special advisor to the secretary-general [Annan] for the Global Compact, helped prepare him for this achievement. As one of the top architects of that earlier UN initiative with business, the Global Compact, he honed skills for operating on the international ideological and political terrain. By the time he took office at the Human Rights Council headquarters in Geneva, it was clear that he wasn't there to save the treaty-based Norms. From the very start, he emphasized the distinctiveness of his mandate. It is "primarily evidence based," he wrote in his first report; but "it inevitably also entails making normative judgments." He called this approach "a principled form of pragmatism: an unflinching commitment to the principle of strengthening the promotion and protection of human rights as it relates to business, coupled with a pragmatic attachment to what works best in creating change where it matters most—in the daily lives of people."

As he and his team went about doing their own survey of the current state of business and human rights, they built a conceptual framework that, unlike the Norms, distinguishes the role of the State from the role of business. So were born the three core principles described in the council-approved framework: 1) *the State duty to protect* against human rights abuses by third parties, including corporations; 2) *the corporate responsibility to respect* human rights; and 3) the obligation of both (and others) to develop better access to remedies for human rights abuses. At least ideally, "the three principles form a complementary whole in which each supports the others in achieving sustainable progress," as Ruggie puts it.

Although the Norms were sidelined, the debate continues about what to do and what not to do and about the dividing line between roles, though not in the highly charged environment that helped doom the Norms. The current mood, quieter and more positive, stems from what Ruggie senses is a widespread realization on all sides that it is urgent to leaven globalization with human rights.

Ruggie and his team advanced that understanding through the diligent and transparent way they worked in the past three years. They held fourteen "multistakeholder" consultations (including large regional meetings in Bangkok, Bogota, and Johannesburg), conducted a survey of Fortune Global 500 corporations, originated more than two dozen other research projects, and generated more than a thousand pages of documentation as the factual and conceptual foundation for their three reports to the council. Ruggie also delivered dozens of carefully prepared speeches and distributed the texts widely to let people know what he was up to. Further, he arranged to have these activities fully documented and open to the public, not only in the UN's archives, but also on the user-friendly Web site of the London-based Business and Human Rights Resource Center, whose staff covers human rights developments on a daily basis.

In the course of these activities, Ruggie paid international business officials the kind of attention they deserve as leaders representing the global dynamo of more than 78,000 multinational corporations and their 780,000 subsidiaries. At the Paris headquarters of the International Chamber of Commerce (ICC) in April 2007, he gave a lengthy summary of his second (February 2007) report ("Mapping International Standards and Responsibility for Corporate Acts") and then participated in an exchange of views that an ICC statement called "rich and constructive." After this kind of give-and-take with organized business, Ruggie's framework won the approval of the Big Three of international organized business: the ICC, the International Organization of Employers (IOE), and the Business and Industry Advisory Committee to the Organization for Economic Cooperation and Development (OECD).

Will these top-level approvals cause corporations to join this initiative? The better question is whether Ruggie's continuing "multistakeholder" endeavors will have a cumulative impact over time. That remains uncertain, but Ruggie salted his reports, speeches, and interviews with a range of reasons why they should climb aboard the UN's human rights express.

Take the case he outlines near the opening of his latest report. After hailing markets as "powerful forces" for progress, he continues,

> But markets work optimally only if they are embedded within rules, customs, and institutions. Markets themselves require these to survive and thrive, while society needs them to manage the adverse effects of market dynamics and produce the public goods that markets undersupply. Indeed, history teaches us that markets pose the greatest risks—to society and itself—when their scope and power far exceed the reach of the institutional underpinnings that allow them to function smoothly and ensure their political sustainability. This is such a time, and escalating charges of corporate-related human rights abuses are the canary in the coalmine, signaling that all is not well.

Ruggie goes to great lengths to analyze the environment in which multinational corporations operate in the twenty-first century. The crucial reality recognized in Ruggie's analysis is that globalization has led to "governance gaps," or "weak governance zones"—areas where few of the underpinnings of law and order exist. In a preview of what he wrote in his subsequent reports, Ruggie told the 2006 World Mines Ministries Forum in Toronto, "This authority vacuum, or governance gap, often leads responsible companies to stumble when faced with some of the most difficult choices imaginable or to try and perform *de facto* governmental roles in local communities for which they are ill equipped. Less responsible firms take advantage of the asymmetry of power they enjoy to do as they will."

In his talks in Toronto and elsewhere, as in his reports, Ruggie repeatedly emphasized that "our fundamental challenge" is to narrow and ultimately to bridge this governance gap. It must be bridged, he added, "by efforts from all sides if companies are to sustain their social license to operate, and if the people of the countries involved are to benefit from the enormous potential contributions that [global industry] can make to economic and social development." He makes a big point about the need for efforts by all sides so that "thinking and action can build in a cumulative way."

In delineating the separate roles of government (the State) and of business in meeting that challenge, Ruggie seems mindful of the loud complaint of business that the Norms would saddle business with governmental obligations. So he is unambiguous about the State's duty to protect human rights. "The human rights regime rests upon the bedrock role of States," he asserts in explaining the first principle of his three-pronged framework and how it is enshrined in domestic and international law. That may not turn out as quite the concession to business that it might seem however.

By listing specifics on how governments fall short in fulfilling their basic duty, Ruggie has in effect written a set of action programs waiting to be incorporated into campaigns. One important example is this: "They [States, or governments] need to consider human rights impacts when they sign trade agreements and investment treaties and when they provide export credit and investment guarantees for overseas projects, especially in contexts where the risk of human rights challenges is known to be high."

Three other items on his list of a "diverse array of policy domains" through which a State may fulfill its human rights duty are the following:

— Improving the effectiveness of the OECD multinational corporation guidelines by making its national "contact points" more responsive in settling complaints
— Strengthening the capacity of the courts to hear complaints and enforce remedies against corporate misbehavior
— Redefining fiduciary duties, as the United Kingdom has done recently, to require corporate directors to "have regard" to

matters such as "the impact of the company's operations on the community and the environment"

Ruggie's second principle—the corporate responsibility to protect human rights—is founded on "the basic expectation society has of business," which he restates as "do no harm" but with a positive accent: doing no harm "may entail positive steps—for example, a workplace antidiscrimination policy may require the company to adopt specific recruitment and training programs."

In a special study of more than three hundred reports of alleged corporate-related abuses, he found that the "do no harm" principle applies to a surprising range of corporate behavior. The empirical study identified violations of twelve labor rights and seventeen nonlabor rights. In other words, "there are few if any internationally recognized rights [that] business cannot impact—or be perceived to impact—in some manner." Ruggie concludes that there are no limits to the rights that companies "should take into account" (whereas the Norms contain only "a limited set of rights for which [a corporation] may bear responsibility").

Consequently, Ruggie winds up laying a potentially heavy human rights burden on corporations. It is one that can be met, he says, by exercising the moral and legal requirement of "due diligence." Ruggie defines due diligence for human rights as having four necessary elements: written policies, integration of those policies throughout a company, impact assessments (before new activities are launched), and tracking performance. Due diligence, Ruggie points out, can help a company rebut a charge of "complicity"—meaning a company's *indirect* involvement in human rights abuses, where the actual harm is done by another party, including governments and nonstate actors. He warns that a truthful defense "that a company was following orders, fulfilling contractual obligations, or even complying with national law will not, alone, guarantee it legal protection."

Here Ruggie sees a useful role for the UN Global Compact, the business and human rights project that he helped found and develop. With more than 2,300 participating companies (making it "by far the world's largest corporate social responsibility initiative"), the Global Compact is "well positioned" to help companies and their industries adopt, refine, and standardize their due-diligence practices. According to Ruggie's findings, "relatively few companies have systems in place to support claims that they respect human rights."

No wonder that one international law firm, Wachtell, Lipton, Rosen & Katz, in a May 1 memo to its corporate clients, objected to the Ruggie report because it would "impose on corporations the obligation to compensate for the political, civil, economic, social, or other deficiencies of the countries in which they conduct business"—a point strikingly similar to one made by the U.S. Council of International Business nearly five years ago. In a rebuttal, another titan of the New York bar, Weil, Gotshal & Manges, argued that the best U.S. companies already monitor human rights as part of their fiduciary duties and that for all companies Ruggie's rules simply restate existing legal requirements.

Which legal opinion is right? Both, in a sense. The Ruggie report apparently does not introduce any new legal requirements, but it carefully documents and spells out existing ones and thereby adds to pressures on corporate boards and corporate lawyers to beef up their human rights policies. For that reason, a coalition of socially responsible investors announced on June 11 that they support the Ruggie report. Still, some influential human rights organizations insist Ruggie do more. On May 20 they went public with their view that a follow-up mandate for Ruggie should "include an explicit capacity to examine [specific] situations of abuse . . . to give greater visibility and voice to those whose rights are negatively affected by business activity." For the business representatives, however, that was unacceptable—they argued it would distract Ruggie from his mandate to "operationalize" the framework.

Professor Ruggie will almost surely not assume the role of prosecuting attorney against a Nike or Wal-Mart, but it will be hard for him to avoid studying how specific companies—those with a brand name to protect and those without one—fail to address human rights abuses for which they are directly or indirectly responsible.

Under his new mandate, Ruggie will have to be careful not to neglect the third principle of his framework, the obligation to respond to the need for improving access to remedies for human rights violations. In his reports, he lists the mechanisms for redress already available in treaties, domestic law, industry agreements, and various other arrangements, not so much to record achievements, but to inventory the opportunities waiting to be seized and enlarged.

Overall, Ruggie's most difficult challenge comes from those "weak governance zones" that rightly worry him—the areas where the government is unable or unwilling to exercise its authority and where multinationals have expanded and prospered. Recognizing the urgency of filling this vacuum, he has put all options on the table, including home state regulation of the multinational corporation's foreign operations. Traditionally, that option is a big No-No. Based on extensive research of current legal opinion, however, Ruggie finds change is in the wind. This is the evolving consensus that he discovered: international law does not *require* home states to regulate the conduct of their multinationals abroad, but does not flatly *prohibit* it (in other words, *permits* it under certain circumstances), and moreover, some treaty bodies (the UN entities that interpret the UN treaties) are leaning toward *encouraging* such regulation.

The first government that is likely to take advantage of that latitude is Australia's, whose multinationals have not all been models of rectitude overseas. In June 2008 the parliament, giving credit to Ruggie for the idea, adopted a motion calling for "the development of measures to prevent the involvement or complicity of Australian companies that may result in the abuse of human rights." It was a statement of intent, but this intent is one that the United States, with a much larger stake in the global economy, would be wise to make its own.

So, all things considered, where do we stand in the struggle for human rights?

Thirteen years ago, I wrote, "When it comes to the rights of working men and women, international commerce today is still at a primitive stage: lawless and amoral. Almost anything goes." Incredibly, that is still true.

At several points during those thirteen years, something happened to persuade me that we were at a turning point—that we were making a breakthrough in the struggle against sweatshops and for a global system that grants the rights of working men and women the respect that business and business people have long taken for granted for themselves. But I was too optimistic. I was wrong each time. Sweatshops continued to flourish. Worse, sweatshops lived on in the business culture, not seriously challenged as an acceptable way of doing business.

Now, thanks to the Human Rights Council's adoption of Ruggie's paradigm, there is reason for renewed optimism. As Ruggie correctly emphasizes, "The international community is still in the early stages of adapting the international human rights regime to the challenges posed by globalization." True, but even in the early stages, we have, in my view, seen a significant advance because of the new agreed-upon framework for business and human rights. The challenge for governments, corporations, human rights organizations, unions, investment firms, and other "stakeholders" is to work together to exploit the vast potential that the new paradigm offers.

* * *

As I was drafting this chapter, I got an e-mail from Neil Kearney, the general secretary of the global union for garment and shoe workers. Oddly, it was marked SPAM, but it was nothing of the sort. I opened it immediately because of its subject: Bangladesh.

Although I hardly ignore Bangladesh in this book, I have paid too little attention to it of late in my recent Web reports. The e-mail refocused my attention. It highlighted Kearney's testimony to the ILO committee on the application of standards and the action that the committee took. "Garment workers in Bangladesh, mainly women, cannot be allowed to drop further into serfdom," Kearney told the committee. "The ILO cannot let Bangladesh drive trade unions out of existence."

After recalling the ILO committee's criticism of the government's policies in June 2006, he said that conditions have worsened since then. Trade union activity has been outlawed. "As direct result, worker exploitation has intensified and, in the absence of worker representation, near anarchy prevails because of frequently late payment of wages, cheating on overtime pay, and physical abuse of workers."

I cleared my computer desk of all materials except Kearney's six-page e-mail of June 6. I quickly wrote and posted an article that summarized his detailed testimony, with an e-mail link to his Web site (www.itglwf.org) for the full text. I ended the article as follows:

> Accordingly, the committee censured Bangladesh, as it has many times before [in the past twenty years]. Once again, Bangladesh offers evidence that U.S. trade legislation needs to be strengthened to protect the rights of hundreds of thousands of women workers in Bangladesh, who are essentially part of our labor force. Who cares?

To which I now add, *Who cares enough to make sure that those responsible are finally held accountable?*

Colonialism in Modern Garb

(Compiled from various issues of Human Rights for Workers, starting with volume I, number 1, of February 11, 1996)

IN THE ABSENCE of strong commitments to human rights on the global level, a new form of colonialism has spread through much of the world. In the modern model, you move your business from your democratic home country to a foreign country that puts very few or no limits on how you can exploit its workers. In this environment (call it a "weak governance zone"), your position of power enables you not just to profit from low wages but also to take advantage of the weakness of the typical worker, usually a woman, in many other ways:

- You can make her work ten to twelve hours a day, six or seven days a week, without holidays.
- You can fire her for joining a union or for any other reason or for none at all, often without even paying her the wages still due her.
- You can endanger her health and even her life in an unhealthy or unsafe workplace.
- You can swear at her and beat her if she makes a mistake.

Moreover, when you can take your business from a country like the United States and put it in a country whose government guarantees that you will be *union free,* you can also benefit from other "freedoms," such as

- freedom from sexual harassment lawsuits,
- freedom from antidiscrimination laws,
- freedom from health and safety regulations,
- freedom from limitations on overtime,
- freedom from labor inspectors,
- freedom from equal pay for equal work requirements,
- freedom from courts that enforce the law,
- freedom from environmental restrictions, and
- freedom from many other worker rights protections devised by law and custom in democratic societies.

CHAPTER 23

Keeping Pace with the 21ˢᵗ Century

Numbers by themselves throw little light on the world as it is, as it has changed, and as it should be. To be properly understood, numbers need context, the kind offered by analytical concepts or analytical tools. Here I describe and evaluate five[1] of them, some of which that I have employed, explicitly or implicitly, in some preceding chapters. I also summarized two of them in book reviews reprinted in the "Global Insights" chapter.

WHILE TAKING A postgraduate course in sociology at the University of Chicago many years ago, I had a teacher, Professor William Ogburn, who pioneered a theory of social change that has applications today. In the process of modernizing, according to Ogburn, societies experience *cultural lags*, in which the modernizing sector grows out of sync with the rest of the culture. The spread of new technology,

---

[1]   Without implying that the five are the only useful ones contained in intellectual tool kits. An important omission here, as elsewhere in the book, is *moderation*, as an analytical criterion to be applied to excessive CEO compensation, the credit card binge, and the massive public debt, for example.

which played the key role in Ogburn's formulation, outpaces other parts of culture and usually causes tensions until the culture adjusts to it.

An example in his classroom discussion was, and in real life still is, the division of labor between men and women. Labor-saving technology in the kitchen and elsewhere in the home "greatly reduced the time, effort, and skill needed for housekeeping, but ideas about what wives and mothers should do changed more slowly," as a later sociologist, Alex Thio, explained this example of Ogburn's cultural lag.

Yet even as his student, I couldn't fully accept the exclusive and near-mechanical role that Ogburn assigned to technology. Feminist ideas, antidiscrimination legislation, and wartime labor shortages are among the nontechnological factors that changed woman's role in modern society. My mother, who had once washed the family clothes by hand with a washboard, went to work in a defense plant during World War II because of job openings there. Her factory income enabled her to replace an old washing machine.

Apart from particulars, however, the concept of *cultural lag* is a useful way to map the ways and byways of societal change. In our day, it can illuminate the lag in adjusting the habits and institutions born in the mid-twentieth century to life in the early twenty-first century. Take this example.

The global labor force has doubled since 1980, according to an estimate that Richard B. Freeman, professor of economics at Harvard, made in 2005. He attributed that startling increase to the fact that, since the end of the cold war, countries with huge working populations—China, India, and the former Soviet Union above all—are no longer outside the global economy. Two years later, the International Monetary Fund came up with a more startling estimate: that the global labor force actually *quadrupled* between 1980 and 2005. (Whereas Freeman compared raw labor force data, the IMF compared the *effective* global labor supply of the two periods.)

Whatever the figure, it is a fact that the size of the global labor force has exploded. Many, many more workers around the world now find themselves in the international labor market competing against each other, whether they know it or not. But policymakers are blind to the implications of this historic trend. Nationally and internationally, they are applying global trade and investment principles in the same worker unfriendly pattern adopted in the middle of the last century. Even a powerful backlash against globalization has so far failed to stir governments into effective action, either singly or in concert, to establish global labor policies that fit the new environment.

Although cultural lag is a useful tool for analyzing how, and how well, we adjust to change, it is not the only one. Let me highlight four others:

Francis Fukuyama, John Hopkins University professor of international political economy, outlines another one in his book *America at the Crossroads*. In a chapter on "Rethinking Institutions for World Order," he writes, "As a result of more than two hundred years of political evolution, we have a relatively good understanding of how to create institutions that are rule bound, accountable, and reasonably effective in *vertical solos* we call states. What we do not have are adequate mechanisms of *horizontal accountability* among states" (italics mine).

He makes the same point in another section of his book, but with partly changed imagery: "We do not now have an adequate set of horizontal mechanisms of accountability between the *vertical stovepipes* we label states—adequate, that is, to match the intense economic and social interpenetration that we characterize today as globalization."

In other words, nation-states, whether labeled silos or stovepipes, are not equipped to deal with today's world by themselves. Nor, according to Fukuyama, are the international institutions that they have so far created. He criticizes the United Nations because "it places no practical demands on its members to be democratic or to respect the human rights of its citizens." Moreover, he regards the UN and its allied agencies as largely beyond reform and thinks they should be supplemented (if not replaced) by a set of institutions with greater legitimacy and efficiency.

Whether or not Fukuyama's critique of the UN is accurate, his analytical imagery—a multitude of *vertical* structures and a paucity of *horizontal* ones—helps show why we need international organizations geared to deal with twenty-first-century realities.

Another useful analytical tool is developed in *Global Public Policy: Governing without Government?* by Wolfgang H. Reinicke, formerly a senior fellow with the Brookings Institution, senior economist at the World Bank, and now director of the Global Public Policy Institute, headquartered in Berlin. Reinicke's analysis of the world economy leads him to differentiate globalization sharply from economic interdependence because globalization "denotes radical, sweeping transformation" of the world economy.

According to a widespread contrary view, however, "globalization is not a new phenomenon," as a WTO report states; rather, it is a continuation of a trend of internationalization going back to the 1850s. That view is fundamentally wrong, with serious policy repercussions, Reinicke argues:

> If globalization means faster but still incremental change, there is little need or incentive for governments to reassess either their own role or that of institutions and principles that have governed the world economy since the end of World War II. If instead globalization denotes radical, sweeping transformation, it must be possible to differentiate between interdependence and globalization not only empirically but at a more formal, conceptual level. Such a differentiation would provide the foundation upon which policymakers could reassess the role of government and governance under conditions of globalization.

Reinicke explains that differentiation in great detail. Most of his book goes on to offer thoughtful ideas on how to respond to globalization as a brand-new reality. He prescribes a form of

—

"global governance" (not global *government*) built around sectoral "transgovernmental networks," in which government officials are supplemented with corporate and other nongovernmental representatives from the same sectors. These "public private partnerships," which would include people from the private sector with a direct stake in the outcome, will, among many other advantages, provide "better information, knowledge, and understanding . . . of increasingly complex, technological-driven and fast-changing public policy issues." However, "governing the global economy *without* governments is not an option." The business community, of course, already actively participates in making public policy. It is called lobbying. Reinicke's alternative would make that participation open and transparent and would widen participation to include others with stakes in the outcome.

Reinicke's main contribution is to throw light on how globalization differs radically from internationalization. The policy implications of that fact are yet to be sufficiently understood. After the 2008 Wall Street debacle gripped the United States and the world, however, policymakers finally started an urgent search for global answers in the finance and banking sector.

Another concept that helps illuminate globalization is *governance gaps,* meaning areas in which a government (such as China's) is unable or unwilling to exercise its authority to regulate the conduct of corporations, particularly multinational corporations. Governance gaps, or weak governance zones, is a key concept in a new three-year United Nations project seeking to make the UN Universal Declaration of Human Rights more universal in the policies and practices of the multinational corporations.

"The international community is still in the early stages of adapting the human rights regime to provide more effective protection to individuals and communities against corporate-related human rights harm." That sentence opens a report that led the UN Human Rights Council to approve an ambitious project on human rights and business in mid-2008. Two paragraphs later, John Ruggie, the UN secretary-general's special representative on human rights and business and the project director, wrote,

> The root cause of the business and human rights predicament today lies in the governance gaps created by globalization—[gaps] between the scope and impact of economic forces and actors and the capacity of societies to manage their adverse consequences. Those governance gaps provide a permissive environment for wrongful acts by companies of all kinds without adequate sanction or repair. How to narrow and ultimately bridge the gaps in relation to human rights is our fundamental challenge.

In remarks to the National Roundtable on Corporate Social Responsibility held in Montreal in November 2006, Ruggie applied the concept to the international level, essentially in accord with the judgments of Reinicke and Fukuyama but with a different conceptual metaphor:

> Indeed, the entire international community can be described as a weak governance zone. Markets and transnational corporate networks treat the globe as a single space of transaction flows. In contrast, governance remains anchored in territorially fixed places, with a thin overlay of international law and institutions operating among them, unable on their own to redress human rights abuses, whether corporate or otherwise.

Finally, what about *fairness* as an economic concept? Does it have a place in judging economic policies and practices?

Not according to N. Gregory Mankiw, professor of economics at Harvard and former chairman of the Council of Economic

Advisers under President George W. Bush. "Fairness is not an economic concept," Mankiw wrote in his July 15, 2007, column in the *New York Times* business section. "If you want to talk fairness, you have to leave the department of economics and head over to philosophy."

Outside of academia, however, people don't compartmentalize life that way. "In the real world," as I commented on my Web site at the time, "people are often led to believe that judgments of economists have normative value. So, in accordance with Mankiw's cautions, [the ideas of economists] ought to carry a label like this: *WARNING:* This statement is purely economic, not about fairness or unfairness."

Not all economists agree with Mankiw's value-free perspective. A major dissenter is Joseph E. Stiglitz, professor of economics at Colombia University and winner of the 2001 Nobel Prize in Economics. He states his position most clearly in his book on a controversial subject, *Fair Trade for All,* coauthored with Andrew Charlton, research officer at the London School of Economics. Subtitled *How Trade Can Promote Development,* the book essentially asks and answers the question "What would fair trade agreements look like?"

They set down four basic principles for such an agreement: First, it should be carefully designed to promote, not hinder, economic development. (As things stand, "there is surprisingly little economic analysis of the precise consequences" that an agreement would have.) Second, the agreement should be fair in substance. Third, it should be arrived at fairly, e.g., negotiations should be open and transparent. Last, it should include only "trade-related and development-friendly issues"—not, for example, the protection of patents, copyrights, and other forms of intellectual property rights.

It is not surprising that trade negotiators and their political bosses have not embraced the Stiglitz/Charlton position. In its ideals, *Fair Trade for All* is 180 degrees opposite to the hard-nosed, mercantilist bargaining that has long marked trade negotiations.

Back in 1990, economist John Williamson, in a classic article defining the prevailing free trade strategy dubbed the Washington Consensus, made no direct or indirect mention of fairness or equity. That was because, as he later explained, he found Washington policymakers "essentially contemptuous of equity concerns."

Under various guises, that is still the prevailing mindset of academic economists and of economists in government. Yet the world around them is changing. The old ways have so far caused a stalemate in the Doha negotiations. Public unhappiness with globalization, as shown in poll after poll and at the ballot box, has prompted a rethinking even among some influential economists. The new UN project on business and human rights may help enlarge the narrow mindset.

Another positive sign is that the moral principles in the 1948 UN Declaration of Human Rights are now, more than ever before, a part of public discourse. Those principles are not self-enforcing, of course. A robust effort is required to make them relevant to today's culture, the culture of the twenty-first century, rather than that of 1948.

That is also true of the ILO Declaration of Fundamental Principles and Rights at Work, adopted in 1998 as "a social minimum at the global level to respond to the realities of globalization." Those minimums, and the minimalist way that they have been implemented, fall short of twenty-first-century needs.

CHAPTER 24

Globalization and Us

PERHAPS I SHOULD wind up this book with a ringing call for action. You may well feel such an appeal superfluous if you've read all that has gone before this. In any case, I close with fifteen propositions, short and not too complicated, that dissect the globalization issues confronting us. They also summarize the main themes of this book.

I started formulating the propositions in the May 2007 issue of Human Rights for Workers under the title "5 Points on the Sorry State of Globalization." That title gave the impression that I am an enemy of globalization, when I am not. I *am* opposed to some crucial features of the *present form* of globalization. It has transformed the world economy so rapidly that we have yet to make (and even fully understand) all the changes needed to adjust to the twenty-first century. After further reflection, I decided to take a positive approach by compiling a list of basic ideas about making the world economy serve the common good. I can't, and don't, claim that I discovered those ideas; I have mined the ideas of others, whom I credit throughout the book, with ample quotations from the original sources.

Here is the latest version of the list, obviously with no assumption that it is written in stone. The fifteen propositions are largely empirical in nature and so can be examined and debated on that basis. The exceptions, the ones that are moral or ethical in nature, of course need to be argued on that basis.

1. In transforming the world economy, globalization has created a new dimension—a vast open space of human activity, an international marketplace—outside the traditional jurisdiction of nations and their laws.

2. To establish the rule of law in that open space, governments have created—and are still expanding—a global network of bilateral, regional, subregional, plurilateral, and multilateral agreements laying down cross-border rules on trade, services, investments, intellectual property, and other commercial issues, and have delegated enforcement powers to intergovernmental agencies, with the World Trade Organization at the pinnacle.

3. That global rule of law, however, is only partial, in two senses—*partial* as in incomplete and *partial* as in favoring the rights and interests of one group over others.

4. In its present partial form, globalization protects and promotes the rights and privileges of commerce and capital (particularly multinationals headquartered in the United States, Western Europe, and Japan) to the neglect of labor (the men, women, and children who find themselves in the greatly expanded international labor market).

5. Those procapital rights and privileges, as written, interpreted, and enforced, are balanced by no—or by very ineffective— matching responsibilities or accountability, thereby creating a huge global imbalance.

6. That imbalance leads to an imbalance of power that advances the interests and multiplies the wealth of multinational corporations and allied elites to the disadvantage of other "stakeholders" in all countries, particularly the many millions of vulnerable working men, women, and children, as well

as the poor communities that are deprived of the means to protect their own rights and interests.

7. The imbalance is wrong, grievously and glaringly so, and is increasingly understood as wrong, thanks to improved global communications and the proliferating nongovernmental groups committed to correcting inequities—twin developments that are the happy products of globalization.

8. Since globalization itself demonstrates conclusively that the well-being of people can be improved, those now left out are less and less willing to accept their deprived status and often see themselves as sacrificial lambs to further enrich those already fabulously wealthy.

9. Explosive consequences seem more and more likely if the rightful demands for justice continue to be ignored.

10. Risks have multiplied for the most visible manifestation of globalization—multinational corporations, which at latest count number about 79,000 firms, plus 790,000 foreign affiliates, as well as uncounted millions of suppliers in almost every corner of the globe.

11. There is a serious gap between the scope and impact of multinationals, on the one hand, and the capacity of less developed countries to deal with the conduct (and misconduct) of foreign firms.

12. Since the U.S. government, under both Democratic and Republican administrations, took the lead in determining the unbalanced rules of globalization, and in creating the intergovernmental institutions of globalization, it has the responsibility to review those rules and institutions and to upgrade them so that they address the needs of the twenty-first century.

13. That process of review and reform needs to cover the full range of international policies now grouped together under "trade," including significant areas that are not really trade issues—the protection of intellectual property rights, for

example—but that may well contribute more to global inequities than ordinary trade does.

14. The heart of the reform movement should be to make the Universal Declaration of Human Rights more universal in international business, with close attention to the rights of workers, particularly the rights of women workers, who are more vulnerable to exploitation than are men.

15. Integrating social responsibility into trade rules and into intergovernmental trade agencies is absolutely necessary, but it is no cure-all; many other types of private and governmental initiatives are also necessary, particularly to guarantee worker-friendly practices where people actually work.

In a real sense, those fifteen propositions mark high points in my long personal journey of exploration into how to achieve human rights for workers in the expanding global economy. My own thinking on globalization has evolved, as should be evident from my writings in this book. I hope that *Justice at Work* will stimulate the thinking of readers and advance their efforts to make sure that globalization serves people, rather than the other way around.

Managing Globalization

GLOBALIZATION IS A reality present today in every area of human life, but it is a reality which must be managed wisely. Solidarity too must become globalized.

—*Pope John Paul II in an address on May 1, 2000, to two hundred thousand people from more than forty countries*

INDEX